Repeat 1st 11 bars
= 107 bars then
proceed
rall.
Repeat
bars
73–80
rall.
8va
rall.
ff

Unfinished Symphonies

Close-up of Rosemary Brown's hands on the Liszt composition entitled Grübelei (Pondering).

UNFINISHED SYMPHONIES

Voices from the Beyond

Rosemary Brown

Foreword by The Bishop of Southwark

William Morrow and Company, Inc., New York 1971

Printed in the United States of America.
Library of Congress Catalog Card Number 78-151911

CONTENTS

Foreword

by

THE BISHOP OF SOUTHWARK

Rosemary Brown lives within fifteen minutes walk of Bishop's House on the other side of Tooting Bec Common, but it was not until the spring of 1970, eleven years after I came to the district, that we met. It was at a dinner in Knightsbridge organised by *Psychic News*. There was a large attendance, several hundreds, and one of the items on the programme was a recital by Rosemary Brown. It was a remarkable performance, which attracted the attention of the audience and stimulated interest and discussion. I think it would be fair to say that no matter what the explanation may be, nobody at that dinner would want to question her integrity. She is convinced that she is in touch with Liszt and other great composers. She sees them, talks with them, and becomes a channel for their most recent works. I am not competent to express a technical judgment on the quality of the music but some who are better informed than I are satisfied that what is written down is in the style of the composers—in short it "rings true". Now if Rosemary Brown had devoted her life to music and was a brilliant pianist it might be possible to find a straightforward explanation. But that is not the case. Rosemary Brown grew up in comparatively humble circumstances which did not provide money or leisure for the pursuit of musical studies. In more recent years she has been a busy housewife and mother in her home in Balham. As Sir George Trevelyan says, she had no musical background or initial talent, almost no train-ing, and very little experience in listening to records or concerts whether live or on the radio. Her main job, as a widow, was to make ends meet, and this she did by work-ing five hours a day in the school meals service.

In my opinion the most likely explanation of this pheno-menon is a psychic one. It is to be found in Rosemary Brown's mediumship. It is a pity that the word "medium" has unfortunate overtones because, in its strict sense, it means nothing more than an intermediary, somebody who acts as a go-between. In this instance, so it would seem, a group of musicians led by Liszt and Chopin, wished to add to their works for the benefit of mankind. They chose Rosemary Brown as their agent.

Of course this explanation will seem absurd to those who reject the concept of a life after death, and they will doubtless resort to the old arguments of 'telepathy' and 'intuition' without defining what they mean by these words. But it is not absurd to people who regard death as a comparatively unimportant event in the development of personality. As one who has been interested in psychical research for many years I believe it reasonable to suppose that on the other side of the grave we discover life in an-other dimension with enhanced powers. If this is so it is also reasonable to suppose that artists will continue to develop their particular gifts. Indeed it would be a curious concept of the next world if those who had struggled creatively while they were here were not to be given the opportunity to practise their crafts.

Why Liszt and this group of composers should choose Rosemary Brown rather than a famous pianist or com-poser is anybody's guess. Perhaps it is another example of the Biblical method whereby Truth is revealed through the humble and unpretentious. The heroes in the Old and

New Testament were distinguished by their integrity, not by their birth or their possessions.

At a time when men's minds are imprisoned by the materialism of their environment and when the Church finds it difficult to point them to a nobler existence, Rosemary Brown's experiences stand out as a challenge and a sign-post for the discerning. There is a world beyond this one and, if we did but know it, we live out our lives in the shadow of eternity.

MERVYN SOUTHWARK

Bishop's House,
38 Tooting Bec Gardens, S.W.16

Unfinished Symphonies

CHAPTER ONE

The Beginning

The first time I saw Franz Liszt, I was about seven years old, and already accustomed to seeing the spirits of the so-called dead.

I was in the top bedroom in the big, old house in London where I still live. That particular morning I remember I had woken early, and was lying there enjoying the warmth of the bed, and waiting to hear my mother's voice call when it was time to get up. She always woke my brothers and me in plenty of time for school—as much as an hour-and-a-half before the time we had to leave, so that we would have the opportunity to wash and dress and eat breakfast without beginning the day in a rush.

Part of the house was let to lodgers in order to bring a little more money to help the family finances, and as a result I had to sleep in my parents' bedroom at that time. The room was an attic with gabled ceilings which reminded me of a church, and because of this gave me a secure feeling.

The furniture was very simple and my bed sat in the corner. It was second-hand and sagged alarmingly in the middle. Even my slight weight would bring the head and the footboards dipping towards each other when I climbed into it.

It was in this almost primitively simple room that Liszt first appeared to me. I was not in the least scared when I saw him standing at my bedside. I had been accustomed to seeing discarnate beings—or spirits as most people call them—since I was a tiny child, so there was nothing frightening about the vision. In fact, I don't think I was even surprised. You take a lot in your stride when you are a child.

He came on that first occasion as a very old man. His long hair was very white and he was wearing what I took to be a long black dress. At seven I didn't know what a cassock was. But I remember thinking it funny that a man should be wearing something like that, though his visit was so brief that I hardly had time to wonder about any of it before he was gone.

For some reason he never said who he was that morning. I suppose he knew I would eventually see a picture of him somewhere and would recognise him. There is, after all, no mistaking Liszt for anyone else, especially when he was an elderly man with long white hair and wearing the sombre robes.

All he said that morning, speaking slowly because I was a child, was that when he had been in this world he had been a composer and pianist.

He then said: "When you grow up I will come back and give you music."

It was all very distinct. A simple statement with no complicated sentences and no long words, framed for a child to understand. He might even have thought his name too difficult for me to grasp at that time. But the whole experience was very, very vivid, and I never forgot him coming or what he had said.

I didn't mention his visit to anyone at the time, mainly because I was so used to seeing people from another world that I never thought much about their arrival unless they said or did something I felt might be important and that I should tell other people.

There seemed no reason to talk about this particular visitation, and it was many years later before he came back to fulfil his promise. And then on a scale that I can still hardly believe to be possible.

Today Liszt is the organiser and leader of a group of famous composers who visit me at my home and give me their new compositions. There are twelve at present in the group—Liszt, Chopin, Schubert, Beethoven, Bach, Brahms, Schumann, Debussy, Grieg, Berlioz, Rachmaninov and Monteverdi. I have placed them in the order in which they communicated. Others, such as Albert Schweitzer, appear briefly and give me a little music then don't seem to return. Mozart, for example has been just three times. But after six years of work I have today, in drawers and cupboards all over my big rambling house, some 400 pieces of music—songs, piano pieces, some incomplete string quartets, the beginning of an opera as well as partly completed concertos and symphonies.

The work involved has been tremendous. I have had a very limited musical education which meant that I was unpractised in the straighforward technicalities of writing down notes, and unacquainted with the knowledge of how to orchestrate; and all the while there has also been the task of keeping in contact with beings from another world—the world of spirit—who sometimes do not come through as clearly as one would wish.

However, much of the music now exists on paper. Some of it is beginning to be heard in public, and in May 1970, just a little more than six years after Liszt communicated with me again, there was launched a long playing record of eight different composers' 'other side' music. The composers themselves were naturally pleased with this breakthrough.

Liszt and the others are not making all these efforts to give me their music for any reasons of vanity. Communication is not always easy for them and there is a definite purpose behind the work which I think can best be explained in the words of Sir Donald Tovey, a very distinguished musician and composer who died in 1940. He is another of my visitors and hopes to dictate a book to me which will be called "Immortality". One night, January 1, 1970 to be exact, when I was having difficulty sleeping, he arrived and said: "Well, as you can't sleep, we may as well do some work."

Rather reluctantly I got out of bed, put on a dressing-gown and sat while he dictated his explanation of the purpose behind the composer's work with me. His intention was that the words should be used on the sleeve of the record as an explanation of the aims and ideals for which we and the others were working.

"Better than you trying to explain," he said, but kindly.

I think his words should be repeated here also. Sir Donald, who was a very distinguished writer in his lifetime makes the intentions behind this astral music clearer than I possibly could.

He dictated "As you listen to this record, you may wonder whether the music you hear is the product of Rosemary Brown's abilities, or whether it has indeed emanated from departed composers who are still creating music in another world. This music itself has already called forth some admiration and some denigration (as almost any music does), but I am happy to note that the former considerably outweighs the latter. I also note that those who denigrate the music usually do so, not as a result of certain exacting standards, but as the outcome of a measure of scepticism.

"Many ideas have been formulated to explain the emergence of the music, but the possibility that composers of the past are still alive in different dimensions from yours, and endeavouring to communicate, should not be dismissed too perfunctorily. Even the most stubborn dis-believers in Extra-Sensory-Perception cannot prove conclusively that there is no life after physical death, and scoffers may one day find themselves faced with indisputable instances of authentic communication from those who have shuffled off their mortal coils.

"Humanity is now moving into an age of increasing emancipation from many of its past limitations. Technical achievements and medical advances confer growing freedom from various oppressions and ills. Man's greatest problem is still himself and his orientation to his fellow-beings. To understand himself fully he should become aware of the fact that he does not consist merely of a temporary form which is doomed to age and die. He has an immortal soul which is housed in an immortal body and endowed with a mind that is independent of the physical brain.

"In communicating through music and conversation, an organised group of musicians who have departed from your world, are attempting to establish a precept for humanity, i.e. that physical death is a transition from one state of consciousness to another wherein one retains one's individuality. The realisation of this fact should assist man to a greater insight into his own nature and potential super-terrestrial activities. The knowledge that incarnation in your world is but one stage in man's eternal life should foster policies which are more farseeing than those frequently adopted at present, and encourage a more balanced outlook regarding all matters.

"We are not transmitting music to Rosemary Brown simply for the sake of offering possible pleasure in listening thereto; it is the implications relevant to this phenomenon which we hope will stimulate sensible and sensitive interest and stir many who are intelligent and impartial to consider and explore the unknown regions of man's mind and psyche.

"When man has plumbed the mysterious depth of his veiled consciousness he will then be able to soar to correspondingly greater heights."

It took Sir Donald Tovey two hours to dictate that to me, and only then was I permitted to go back to bed. But what he wrote, through me, is the explanation to the music—for those who are open-minded enough to accept it. And I do realise that this will not be everyone. Unfortunately there are people who laugh at the work I do without for a moment giving it some serious consideration. I have no wish to be taken pompously nor do I think people should be gullible—obviously everything must be questioned—but some people simply dismiss evidence of life after death with no more than a jeer.

The work I do is fascinating and I have dedicated myself to be the intermediary to the best of my ability, but because of the closed minds in the world there are times when I wish perhaps that someone else had been chosen for the task.

For the last six years it seems that I have been constantly investigated. Even those words of Sir Donald Tovey's were computerised, as it were, to see if the writing patterns corresponded with the work he had done while on earth. The examiner in this case, David Hogarth, a Scottish music critic, writing for *Time and Tide* seemed

pleasingly convinced. He concluded his analysis by saying, "With all due respect to Mrs. Brown, I could not
think for a moment that she had written it herself."

Mention was made in that piece of how Sir Donald
liked to play with words, and I had experience of this myself in the early summer of 1970 when I went to Dublin
to take part in a "live" TV programme.

After some discussion of the music, the programme was
thrown open to the audience to ask questions. Most of the
questions were quite sensible, but one man got up and
said: "I would like to know what Mrs. Brown drinks!"

'Tea, mostly,' and the audience roared with laughter
at both the question and answer.

Tovey was on the platform with me, watching how
things were going and I got a comment from him immediately.

He said: "The audience is 'Dublined' up with
laughter," and I thought, that's typical of him—making
one of his puns.

My words and the music are constantly analysed. The
music has been put through countless tests. I have volun-
tarily taken musical tests, intelligence tests, psychological
tests, psychic tests—every kind of test imaginable, even
apparently irrelevant ones. Professor Tenhaeff, the eminent professor of Parapsychology at Utrecht University,
and his colleagues pronounced me to be quite normal after
they had carried out extensive tests. One musician who
wished to wave away the psychic explanation for the
music, suggested that I had actually had prolonged and
advanced musical training, and then suffered from
amnesia, causing me to forget this alleged training. My
family doctor was able to dismiss this as complete non-
sense, and most of the facts concerning my life can be—
and have been—quite easily and fully checked owing to

the fact that I have lived in the same house all my life. And for this reason, friends, neighbours, relatives and various local authorities can testify to these details.

Those who scoff have to try to furnish some explanation for the music since they cannot dismiss it as non-existant. The music, of course, must be investigated impartially. In fact, I myself am continuing to explore the conditions necessary for effective communication with the world of spirit.

I suppose it was much easier to live with these sometimes inconvenient powers of mine when I was a small child. By the time Liszt came to see me, I had already realised that not everybody saw and heard as I did, and I had learnt that it was wise to be a little discreet about the spirit visitors. When I was very young I used to tell my mother quite a lot of what I saw, but found it sometimes alarmed her. She would say: "How did you know that?", or "You couldn't possibly know that. It happened before you were born."

Sometimes she seemed so concerned that in the end I began to hesitate to tell even her what I had seen and I began keeping the people from the other world to myself.

None of what I saw or heard at that time was of any great importance. It had mostly to do with relations and friends departed from this life and also to do with our old house. I could visualise the house quite clearly as it had been many years before. I knew how the furniture had been placed then, and I could describe items that had been in the house only *before* I was born, when my paternal grandparents (long dead) had lived there.

I could also picture the site of the house in another time completely. I knew how our street had looked before the house had been built. It still happens to me sometimes. I actually see another time and another place. I seem then to be *there,* in it. These are not objective scenes. They are subjective. A third eye picture. And quite different from seeing discarnate spirits. That to me is an objective experience.

In a way it was surprising that my mother was alarmed when I suddenly trotted out my examples of extra-sensory-perception as she herself had second sight, though examples of it occurred very rarely.

Later in life, my mother grew to welcome these indications of life after death, but they did rather disturb her when I was young.

Grandmother had also been psychic, so I suppose the gift does rather run in our family. My mother had what we would call intuition about things. She was half-Scots and very Celtic in many ways, so I suppose that helped, too. I remember her once telling me how one of her flashes of intuition had probably saved her brother's life.

My mother had two brothers, one of whom died in infancy, and when they were children her family were really quite well-to-do. (I'm afraid my poor mother's life changed a lot for the worse in later years.) She would have been living in Putney or Wimbledon at the time where her parents had a beautiful home with enough land to keep chickens and ducks. On this occasion her brother, then very small, was suddenly taken ill. No one could work out what was the matter.

They sent for the doctor who was equally puzzled but said the trouble could be some kind of poisoning. Then my mother had one of her sudden flashes of intuition. The ducks had had something wrong with them and the vet had supplied some pills to cure them. Suddenly my mother *knew* that her brother had taken the pills.

"How many of those ducks' pills did you take?" she asked him, and her mother gave a gasp, realising that

could be the answer. Fortunately the doctor knew the anti-
dote, but he said afterwards that if it hadn't been for that
sudden remark on the part of my mother, her brother
would probably have died.

That was the way it worked with her. She didn't see
very much, but she would get these sudden flashes of
knowledge. Perhaps it worried her when she herself was
young, for otherwise it is hard to understand why my
E.S.P. and clairvoyance did cause her some concern for
a time.

This necessity to keep my thoughts private from my
mother did cause something of a gap between us. I realise
now that I must have seemed reserved, and she seemed, in
a way, remote to me. I know she was fond of me, and I
was most certainly fond of her, but we were not very close
until my mid-teens onward. Then perhaps she felt I was
old enough to be treated as a friend rather than as a child.

She was not very young when I was born—she must
have been about thirty-seven—and as I was the youngest
of the family they actually called me 'Baby' until I was
about 12 when I began to rebel against it.

My contacts with astral beings did not make my childhood particularly easy. It was not only in my mother's
company that I was always having to guard my tongue.
I was very young when I realised that though the visitations I experienced seemed perfectly normal and not in
the least frightening to me, other people did not react the
same way. Attitudes varied from simple disbelief to a
barely concealed conviction that I was a bit mad. I can
accept these extremes of opinion from people now I am
an adult, but when I was a child with a child's sense of
justice, I found other people's disbelief in what was, to
me, a normal and real happening rather hard to understand.

I can't actually remember the very first astral being I saw. There are vague memories that go back to when I was about two. The first visitation that I remember clearly and in complete detail was a very early one. I would have been very young—perhaps six or seven—and I was, of course, sleeping in my parents' bedroom then. The room that was subsequently to become mine had been let off for much-needed money. Things were very difficult financially at that time and we all packed into as few rooms as possible and let the remainder of the house.

Again it was early morning when I woke up. I was lying on my back and staring up at the ceiling, and I'm afraid this is going to sound very romantic and imaginative. But, it did happen. I saw what appeared to be a knight in beautiful shining armour standing over me with a sword held upright above his head. He was so beautiful and there was such an air of peace and calm about him that I could not possibly have been in the slightest degree frightened. I felt certain he was some kind of guardian angel standing over me (perhaps we do all have guardians without being aware of them) and I felt happy and protected for the rest of the day.

I rarely tell that particular story because it does sound so imaginative and just the kind of vision a child might have. Yet years later I read in the *Psychic News* that a very famous medium, Estelle Roberts, who passed over quite recently, had a very similar experience.

If I do tell about that visitation, some people immediately say that I must have seen pictures of guardian angels in children's books and imagined it all.

As it happens, the only religious picture we had in the house was one of Christ on the cross, and a very gloomy looking thing with a horrible dark background it was. I hated it because it looked so dark and sad, but it had probably belonged to my grandparents. Eventually the frame distintegrated and I was not sorry to see the picture go from the house.

Nor was my home the type to have many children's books. And I was not brought up to go to church or to Sunday school. The only orthodox action from a religious viewpoint on my parents' part was to have me christened in the local Parish church, and my mother taught me a few prayers. They were not churchgoers themselves, so there was no question of forcing me to read the Bible or go to Sunday school. Both my parents believed that no one should be brought up exclusively in any one particular religion. They felt children should be allowed to grow up without being conditioned into any kind of belief, so that when they were adult they could make their own decisions about religion.

My mother, though, was quite devout in her own way. My father was not at all, though towards the end of his life, mainly because of certain manifestations of my E.S.P., he did change his mind to a great extent.

The E.S.P. enabled me to see and hear many of my father's friends who had gone over, and they supplied details about themselves which I could not possibly have known, and I would pass these on to my father when they wished it.

He did not take a great deal of notice at first—I think he probably assumed that I had been listening to family talk and stored up in my subconscious mind the memories of what had been said. But when I received a message from someone called 'Black Alec' for him, he was startled into believing me.

Apparently Black Alec had been something of a black sheep, which accounted for the nickname. He had been a friend of my father's when they were both in their twenties, but Black Alec had pulled some shady deal on my father and from then on the friendship had ended, and my father had completely put him out of mind.

My father had his faults in his lifetime, but he was fanatically honest and could not bear any sort of behaviour which he felt was not straight.

Black Alec had not died in any particularly dramatic circumstances, but he came through to me because he wanted to apologise to my father for the harm he had done him when on earth. I dutifully passed on the message.

My father was astounded by this. The man had died before I was born; even my mother knew nothing of him, and when I gave my father a full description of the man and told him of the apology this seemed to clinch the whole question of my E.S.P. and life after death as far as he was concerned.

After that he was convinced that my visions were not just childish fantasies, and his whole attitude changed.

This happened when I was in my early teens, but I was always very grateful that my parents did not give me any kind of formal religious education because it meant that I could think freely for myself once I had grown up. It also meant that I had not been moulded into dogmatic or narrow-minded concepts.

I didn't actually acquire a Bible until I was quite a lot older—I think when I was about twelve or thirteen and at Grammar School. Most of the girls at school with me automatically went to Sunday school and they decided I should go too, so they took me along with them.

I went to see what it was all about, and the teacher, horrified by my ignorance of the Bible, promptly gave me one. I decided that since I now owned the Book I would read it . . . from beginning to end. I did, and it took me months. There was a lot in it which I couldn't accept, and a lot which even then I felt must be allegorical, but the teachings of the New Testament did from then on form the basis of my religious thinking.

And all this time I continued to see spirits. Looking back I believe that in one way the gift was stronger when I was a child. I saw so much more vividly than I do now —the beings were so real that I could mistake them for someone who was here in the flesh. Nowadays they are not so solid in appearance, though not transparent in the way people imagine ghosts. I suppose the change came because as one gets older one gets all sorts of strange 'blockages of the mind', and powers accepted unquestioningly as a child do not function quite so smoothly.

On the other hand my visitors were not quite so frequent when I was young. I was too busy with school and getting on with growing up. Also I had a lot of homework and housework to do. I believe children were usually brought up to help then, and in our great rambling house there was more to do than in most homes. I had very little time to myself, and the visitations tended to be pushed away because my mind was so very occupied with other things. In retrospect I think it was probably a very good thing that the other world did not occupy too much of my thinking until I was old enough to think things out for myself more fully.

However, there are the odd incidents which stick in the memory. Particularly two occasions when I remember being a little startled myself by an unexpected visitation.

I woke up in the middle of the night and it was very dark in the room. Only the faint streaks of light from the street lamp outside gave any form to the surroundings. In this small glow I could see the figure of a very tall man standing beside my bed and looking down at me. Now my father was rather short and slight, so I knew it couldn't be him. I sat up in bed, my heart thumping, thinking: "Oh —a burglar!"

For the moment I was genuinely scared, but as I sat up the figure vanished. I sighed with relief, said to myself: "Oh—it's only another old ghost," turned over and went back to sleep reassured.

On another occasion I woke—and was perfectly wide awake—in the grey light of an early dawn. I was looking around the room wondering what time it was when I suddenly caught sight of a woman standing by me. She was of a very different build from my mother who was very small and rather plump. This woman was much taller. I had a small moment of panic, wondering who it was and how she had got into the room—she looked far too solid to be a ghost. But then she, too, vanished, and left me relieved to find it had not been an earthly person.

I was then, and I suppose still am, more nervous of the living than those whom people call the dead. I felt very little emotion at seeing astral beings when I was a child. They seemed completely natural to me. I realised that I had experiences not familiar to most other people, but I also realised there were some other people with the same sort of powers. This was fortunate as I might have felt very lonely indeed had I believed I was the only one to see spirits. Yet even so there were times when I felt isolated from other children because I felt that 'seeing' made me different.

If I sometimes told friends about myself I found that the results were not always favourable, I remember when I first went out to work in the Civil Service there were two girls I was friendly with, and I suppose my E.S.P. came up in casual conversation about spiritual matters. I might even have been trying to give them a little insight into the life after death. They were decidedly apprehensive and when I described some of the things I could see and hear connected with them—all of which turned out to be accurate—they were quite upset.

One said: "You're too far-seeing, thank you!"

The other said crossly: "You know too much."

And after that I thought I had better keep my mouth shut.

Often in life my clairvoyance, intuition, E.S.P., mediumship—call it whatever you like, has put me in an awkward position. Having this extra eye has always meant that I knew things I really had no normal means of knowing. At school and when I was in my early teens if I made a slip and betrayed some of this extra knowledge, people would say with great suspicion: "How did you know that?" And I could never explain without having to say that I had access to information by other than normal means.

I remember when I was about thirteen and at grammar school I had been made games captain and was in charge of the keys for the lockers where the netballs and other pieces of sports equipment were kept. I didn't have the keys in my possession all the time, but I was basically responsible for them, and if I loaned them out to any of the other girls, I was meant to remember exactly to whom.

One day the keys went missing. We couldn't find them anywhere. We searched high and low, but it seemed hopeless. I couldn't quite remember who ought to have them, and though I had a fairly shrewd idea which girl I had given them to, she categorically denied ever having mislaid the keys.

Looking back I can see it was a fairly small matter, but at the time there was the most terrific fuss and bother. I suppose the headmistress thought that losing the keys showed a lack of responsibility and care on my part. I felt it really wasn't my fault if I'd loaned the keys to someone who had then lost them, but nevertheless as games captain, I was held responsible.

Several days went past and I was thinking about the missing keys one morning and quite suddenly I just knew where they were. I said to one of the other girls: "Those keys are on the top of the tall cupboard."

We went to look, and sure enough, there they were— right on the top of a very high locker. Feeling quite triumphant I rushed off to tell the headmistress that they had been found.

To my dismay, she was furious. She said: "So you knew all the time they were on top of that cupboard?"

Completely taken-aback, I said I hadn't known. "But I did just suddenly know they were there," I added, and it must have sounded pretty lame.

"How could you 'just suddenly' know they were there?" she said in a very cold voice. I had no answer. Well, certainly no answer that I could give her without the situation becoming very involved. Even at thirteen I really didn't feel I could say to my headmistress that I had had a flash of pure intuition. For that is exactly what it was. Afterwards when I thought over the incident I did wonder if I myself might have thrown the keys up on to the top of the cupboard and then forgotten about them, That's what a psychologist might suggest had happened. But that theory was disproved afterwards when one of the girls in the form came forward and said she had put them up there, meaning to return them to me later. The girl I had loaned the keys to being in a hurry to get home, had asked this other girl to give them back to me.

I was then exonerated, but the headmistress gave me some very odd looks for some time afterwards.

Still, I was always getting myself into spots of bother by blurting things out. I had to be constantly on my guard to watch my speech so as not to say anything that would commit me. But there were still other ways in which I could get tripped up.

One day in school when I was about fourteen our form-mistress gave us each a postcard and said she wanted us to write an essay about it. Mine was a coloured picture of a church in Italy, and on the reverse side it had a paragraph printed in Italian. I read this paragraph through and somehow I knew what it meant. So I wrote down the English for it.

I had, of course, never learned Italian, nor had I had any contact with Italian people. But somehow I knew what those words meant.

Anyway, at the end of the lesson, I gave in my essay and later the teacher said to me: "I didn't realise you knew Italian."

"I don't," I said, with complete truth.

"But you've translated the wording on the card," she said, "you must know Italian."

"No, I don't," I said, stubbornly sticking to the truth and getting myself deeper into difficulties.

"In that case," she said frostily, "how did you understand what was written?"

"I sort of guessed," I said feebly.

"You sort of guessed!" she said, and was very cross indeed, possibly deciding I was lying.

She was always rather restrained towards me after that.

Curiously, a similar thing happened to my son, Thomas. I had to go to Holland to be tested and questioned by the Professors at the Department of Parapsychology at the

University of Utrecht, because of their interest in my E.S.P., and I took Thomas with me. He was thirteen years of age at the time, and sitting in a room where everyone was speaking Dutch. He said suddenly he could understand everything they were saying, though, of course, he does not speak the language himself.

That is another form of E.S.P.—and the same sort of thing has happened to me since the Italian postcard episode. Sometimes I'll be travelling on the bus or tube and there will be foreigners sitting opposite, talking and suddenly I *know* what they are saying. I don't understand how or why, but I do wonder whether it is some particular kind of E.S.P. or telepathy.

However, during my schooldays, as well as these flashes of intuition or whatever you like to call them, I was still seeing people from a different plane, though at that period musicians didn't seem to figure in it much at all. I would see complete strangers, relatives, people from far back in time—mostly ordinary unknown people whose names would mean nothing today. I did see Beethoven once or twice, and I saw Schubert once. I recognised both of them because by this time I was at grammar school where there were a few pictures and photographs of famous people. And often my visitors very considerately came in clothes and appearance similar to the same period of their lives as the pictures I had seen, which made recognition much easier.

I used to wonder why they came to see me, and decided that they knew I liked music and were just being kind.

Liszt with his message about giving me music when I grew up was almost the only vision who spoke to me when I was a small child. It wasn't until I was a little older that I began to hear my visitors speaking or they began to speak. What I did not know was that all my growing up years, my first days at work, and throughout my marriage, Liszt was watching all the time, waiting in the background, and giving me spiritual guidance without my even beginning to suspect where it was coming from. And life for most of the time was so hard that that spiritual guidance helped to keep me going through the difficult days.

After my husband had passed over, I began to be more aware of Liszt's presence. But there wasn't anything conclusive about it. A few notes of melody or a phrase of music would seep into my consciousness, but it was still very vague and altogether unformed. I could hear the music, and sometimes I'd try to pick it out on the piano, and with Liszt's help, as I now realise, would manage to put together the beginnings of a tune.

But probably he had to wait for the right moment to approach me and begin working, and it wasn't until March 1964 that he found the opportunity to give me music in a more positive way. It was then the curious chain of events which is completely altering my life began.

When my husband died at the end of August in 1961 I was left penniless with our two children aged eight and four-and-a-half to bring up alone. We had always been poor, and my husband had been terribly ill for the eighteen months previous to his death. He had non-alcoholic cirrhosis of the liver and bronchial asthma. The liver complaint would cause bouts of complete blindness which meant I hardly dared leave him alone. His illness had been so prolonged that we had gone through all our small amount of savings which consisted mainly of my marriage gratuity from the Civil Service. We had not realised that under the circumstances we could have applied for National Assistance and retained our small financial reserve. As it was, when he died, I was left with nothing. It was also the middle of the school holidays which meant that I could not go out to work myself immediately. I had to be at home with the children.

I applied for National Assistance and was allotted £4.1.6 (as far as I can recollect) a week to keep the three of us until the widow's pension came through and even then I was not allowed the full amount because my husband's cards were said to be inadequately stamped. And I had to pay back every penny of the national assistance money when the pension commenced.

It was essential to get a job, but one that would enable me to take the children to and from school. I felt that Georgina who was just eight might manage on her own because there was only one road to cross and the lollipop man was always on duty there. But Thomas, at only four-and-a-half could not go alone.

I had put him down for school soon after he was born, and he was due to commence at the age of five. However, because of our circumstances, I was able to get him into the infant's section of the primary school. But he finished half-an-hour before his sister at the Junior School, and I couldn't have him waiting about in all weathers for her to bring him home.

The only answer seemed to be some kind of school work which would fit in with the children's hours. I had hoped for a secretarial job but there was nothing going. They did, however, need someone to work in the kitchen, and, poorly paid as it was, I took it on gratefully.

It was a very difficult time altogether. I was missing my husband dreadfully. For two weeks after he died there was a complete blank, and I felt he had disappeared for ever. Now I realise that my own distress was possibly preventing any communication between us, and also that he had suffered so much illness that he had probably been taken to rest for a period of time.

A few weeks after he had gone, one night when the children were tucked up and asleep, I was trying to compose myself in order to sleep as well. I was sleeping very poorly at the time, and just sitting up in bed trying to relax a little. As it happened I was not even thinking of my husband when suddenly I heard his voice. Now my husband had a most unusual voice. It was very deep and rather booming, and after the children were born he always called me 'Mummy'.

Suddenly I heard the word 'Mummy' quite unmistakably in his voice, but the strange thing was that the sound seemed to be coming from my own solar plexus. Then I saw him quite clearly and distinctly sitting on the side of the bed. He looked young and radiantly healthy—quite different from the man whom I had lost just a few weeks before. At the time of his passing he was painfully thin; almost like a skeleton, and I had been haunted by the memory of his emaciated appearance.

The sight of him, so healthy and happy looking helped me enormously; blotting out the picture of how ill he had been. It was a wonderful thing.

He came again very occasionally after that, but never said very much other than he would watch over me and the children, and that he would always be with us. He told me that the children would do well, and be clever and cause me no trouble at all. And this, too, was a great comfort when I was so worried at being left alone with them and with so little money.

Even so, I found it very hard to recover from his death. For two years I couldn't bear to think about him, as if I did, I would break down. I deliberately pushed him out of my mind, but I felt guilty about it, and occasionally would send out a little thought to him, asking him to understand. This sharp emotional aftermath following his death lasted

two years, and I think that during that time I unintention-
ally stopped him coming to us as much as he would have
liked.

But if either the children or myself were ill, he would
always manifest; making a special effort to show that he
was watching over us.

And I believe that he was very close to Thomas in that
time. As I have said, Thomas was not even five years old
at the time of his father's passing, and yet I would find the
child making all sorts of little repairs about the house
when things broke or went wrong.

"How did you know how to do that?" I would ask him.

"Daddy told me," he would say.

And there was a night when we were all watching television and I saw him in the room. Suddenly he started to
switch the electric light on and off—I suppose to give the
children proof that he was there. They were delighted.

"Ask him to do it again, Mummy," they kept saying.

I see him now and again these days. He doesn't say
much, but appears happy, smiling—and infinitely reassuring.

Immediately after my husband's death before contact
was established, the quiet presence of Liszt was a very
great comfort to me. He was not communicating music,
but he was very much there in the background of my life.
And there were two occasions when he was of real prac-
tical help.

Easter came around and though we were given a small
retaining fee by the school meals' service to cover the holi-
day period, I was at my wits' end to think how to manage
until the new term and full pay commenced.

Liszt then said, most unexpectedly: "I think that perhaps you should try the football pools this week."

It seemed a vain hope and he certainly never gave me

any assistance in filling in the coupon, but to my astonishment back through the post came a dividend of £10, and the problem of finance for the next few weeks was solved.

Again, as Christmas drew near and I was thinking about money for presents for the children and for Christmas food, he again suggested, with a little twinkle that I might just try the pools again.

I took his advice, and this time the dividend was £51 odd. It was, for me, a very big miracle. Particularly as I do not make a practice of filling in football coupons. Nor have I ever done so since. I know it would be a complete waste of time to do so expecting any help from the other world. Perhaps Liszt himself did not know whether I would win, but simply had a "hunch" that I would be lucky. People have often asked me if I can foretell gambling wins. The answer is that I cannot; nor will I ever be able to do so. Had I been able to predict things like that, my own poverty would not have been so severe, but in the normal way the spirit world will have nothing to do with any assistance towards monetary gain.

It was after I had been working in the school kitchens for about three years when the next thing happened to bring me nearer to the music. I had an accident. After the school children had finished their meals, it was part of the job to clear the tables and wash them. There was a rota for us all to take turns in doing this. It was my week for this job and I was just about to do it, armed with a bucket of water and a cloth in one hand and some abrasive in the other, when I slipped on a bit of carrot that one of the children had dropped on the wood floor.

As I fell, I caught my ribs on the sharp corner of a table and I think it knocked me out. First I was walking along, and then I felt myself falling, and the next thing I knew I was on the floor, trying to pick myself up and feeling a great deal of pain. I was sent to the South London Hospital where the casualty department wrapped my middle in plaster, put my arm in a sort of sling and sent me home. I think I had broken two ribs, but as the hospital did not X-ray me I shall never know for sure. All I know is that the pain was excruciating and breathing was a very painful business.

I was off for weeks with instructions not to do too much. This cut out any heavy housework, and with the children at school, time went very slowly. I did some reading and some knitting and one day I thought I'd just amuse myself on the piano to pass the time away. My arm was out of the sling and I didn't think I could do my ribs any harm.

It was that afternoon when Liszt appeared very vividly indeed, standing beside me. And instead of my finding a piece of music and playing it for myself, I found he was guiding my hands at the piano. Music was being played without any effort on my part, and it was music that I had never heard before. The odd thing was that I was so curiously unsurprised by the whole episode. What was happening seemed natural and normal, and I thought to myself: "That's rather lovely music," enjoying the pleasurable sensation of listening to the creation of something which I knew was not of my own creating. Other than those feelings, I thought no more about the afternoon's music. Liszt had not spoken. He had just been there. I was not in any sort of trance—I had seen him in fullest consciousness.

After that he kept coming back and giving me more and more music. The only way I can describe his method then is to say that he took over my hands like a pair of gloves. Without astral assistance I could not play the piano at all well at that time. (What little skill I had acquired I had lost through years without practice.) But with his guidance at that time, something more technically pass-able was heard.

At this early stage I wasn't writing the music down, but after several of these rather dreamlike afternoons, he began to speak to me. Before he put the notes in my head or at my finger-tips, he would tell me the name of the piece we were to play together. And then one day he said: "I have come to fulfil my promise. Do you remem-ber me coming to see you all those years ago when you were a little girl?"

I remembered very well. "But you look younger now," I said.

He just nodded and made no attempt to explain. That was to come much later.

From that moment we began to talk a little more. It wasn't difficult; his gift for communication is so developed that when we are en rapport I find him as easy to under-stand as someone who is still here in the flesh. Naturally I was a little shy with him at first—he had been a famous man in his life-time—and I would just sit and listen to him talking, saying very little myself. He talked mostly about the music he was giving me, and I thought how lovely the pieces were and what a pity it was that other people could not hear them, too.

Suddenly I wanted very much to write them down, but unfortunately that was not such a simple undertaking. I did not have sufficient knowledge of the methods of writ-ing down music, and as I have no pitch, remembering and sorting out the correct notes on the keyboard was ex-tremely difficult.

I realise now that Liszt must have been helping me as unobtrusively as possible when I set about trying to put down the notes in my own way. First I would learn the pattern of notes on the piano that he had used my hands to play. He would play several bars at a time and I would memorise them before we went on to the next part.

So I had the melody on the piano, but not on paper. Then I started to write down the notes, using what recollection I had of my piano lessons years before. There had been a gap of some 12 years since I had played. I knew, of course, something of keys and notes, but a lot of theory I had forgotten and much of it I had never learned at all. There were gaps in my knowledge of musical notation and I must have made many mistakes at the beginning. For example, though I would generally manage to get the correct note, I'd put G sharp where it should have been A flat. Both are, of course, actually the same note on the piano, but I wouldn't be able to distinguish which of the two should be written down.

It was all painfully slow. Then I began to realise I could ask Liszt for help when I was puzzled. This improved the notation a great deal and these days, of course, it is becoming easier as most of the composers usually dictate the music to me now. They tell me when it is a chord and which notes make up the chord. They give me the key signatures and each individual note. It is much simpler this way, although very laborious. I have learned a lot from them and as soon as I could afford it, in the autumn of 1967, I also began to take piano lessons to improve my playing. I gave the lessons up after a time as I felt I should concentrate on the writing out of the compositions.

The chief difficulty with the dictation method is that so many of the notes sound alike B.C.D.E.G. in particular can easily become confused because of the similarity of sound, particularly when communication isn't very clear.

There is also the problem of accents and English. Not all the composers can speak English very well, which means that someone, usually Liszt whose English seems nearly perfect, has to interpret. He is able to speak several languages, though whether he did when he was here, I don't know. Some of them couldn't have spoken any English when they were in this world, but they have obviously made the effort to learn a little over there. (It is strange how it does not always occur to people that if one survives, one can go on learning and therefore learn another language.)

However, it was all much more difficult in the beginning. I suppose that both Liszt and I were having to learn. He to transmit to me, and me to receive from him. And to some extent we were both experimenting—looking for the best way to communicate the music. What actually happens can perhaps be compared with 'radio' transmission and reception. In fact, sometimes when contact is difficult, it is just like listening to a foreign station which keeps fading.

There is less of that problem with Liszt, though. He is by far and away the most efficient communicator, and perhaps that is why he is in control of the group. At least, I am pretty certain that this is his role in the composer's plan.

CHAPTER TWO

Why Me?

People who are suspicious regarding the source of my music and who search to find an explanation other than the true one—which is that it is coming from another plane—nearly always have the same theory. They are convinced that I must have had a very thorough musical education when I was young which I am keeping a deep, dark secret.

They reason that this theory can be the only logical answer to over 400 pieces of music, some of which have now been recorded, and all of which are written in at least a dozen different styles.

Anyone knowledgeable about music realises that I would have to be very nearly a musical genius to have achieved all this alone, but most of the non-musical sceptics do not realise how very difficult it is to compose. Perhaps most competent musicians with a flair for extemporising can take any ordinary song and play it with a classical flavour—though even that would be impossible for me to do as I cannot extemporise at all. But actually *composing* in different composers' styles—well, that is quite another thing.

Though not all of the music I have written down is superb—the composers are limited by *my* limitations at present—and the difficulties of transmission—I would surely have had to be a very brilliant musician indeed to have written all those different styles of music myself.

Another foolish idea is that I hankered after fame. Anyone who knows me will realise the truth of the fact— that I much prefer to live quietly, and out of the public eye. So much so that I wonder why people ever covet fame, as it can be a great burden and a nuisance.

I have discovered that one loses all privacy and is constantly having demands of all kinds made upon one, also having to endure the misery of hostile criticism and denigration. And however many times clear proof of the authenticity of the music, and in many cases, of the messages, has been provided, there are the insatiable persons who will not admit to that proof and wish to go on proving it over and over again.

There was a correspondent of one important American news magazine who had a long interview with me, at a time when I was extremely busy with various appointments. Soon afterwards, he asked to have a further interview, naming a day when I would be in Edinburgh on a five day visit. When he finally accepted it was impossible for me to see him then he sent a letter with a long list of questions which he demanded I should ask of the various composers.

At that time I had not so much as half-an-hour to spare, but I assured him that I would do what I could if I had the time and opportunity. Unfortunately his article was published before I could do anything about the questions—the magazine apparently had to go to press—and I am afraid it made some rather unfavourable comments on the matter.

Any medium, and perhaps any person with enough imagination, will know that to obtain an answer from someone in the spirit world is not like dialing a number and pressing a button in order to hear and be heard. Contact may not be immediately available, and, if it is, the person questioned in the spirit world may not know the answer—or wish to allow himself to be subjected to a series of questions.

Nevertheless, I have been fortunate enough to have sufficient attunement with people in spirit to be able to pose certain questions to them and be given their answers.

Perhaps I have more respect for the composers than others, as I hesitate to bombard them with questions about themselves or their work—feeling it is more polite to allow them to say what *they* wish. But then I am constantly face to face with the composers, and this personal meeting inspires in me a respect—almost a reverence—which one cannot always expect other people to feel.

For instance, I am on a sufficiently friendly basis with Liszt to be able to converse and discuss some matters, but this does not include an attempt by me to scrutinise his personal life or extract information concerning his activities during his life in this world. I do feel that would be impertinent of me. Rather, as I have already explained, we talk about God and the purpose of life, and the possibilities of helping humanity.

Still, if the man from the American news magazine had been able to allow me more time I could eventually have given him the answers to some of his questions. Perhaps it is worth printing them here as the magazine was not able to publish both questions and answers owing to their press dates.

The first question they gave me for Beethoven was: "Please recall as best you can your meeting with the twelve year old Franz Liszt."

I asked Beethoven who told me to reply in the following way: "I cannot recall the meeting with young Franz in great detail although his talent made an unexpected impression upon me. He was then a shock-headed lad with a powerful performance at the keyboard, although his style was then too abrupt and undisciplined for my taste.

"I recognised a strength of purpose in the boy's carriage and deportment together with a capacity for sheer hard work, and my conclusion was that he would rise to great heights as a pianoforte virtuoso when maturity had endowed him with poise and a smoother-flowing technique.

"The concert hall was full of people, the event having been announced well in advance, and I sat at the rear so that I could effect an exit unnoticed should I become bored. Franz seemed a remarkably quiet boy until he sat at the piano and commenced to play, when he became transformed into a demon of energy who shocked the audience and myself into attention. His arms threshed the air like the sails of a windmill; his body leapt about on the piano stool as if it were a spring-board; his hands plunged down on to the keyboard with a ferocity which sometimes shook his slight frame. But in spite of his wild gestures, there was no mistaking his co-ordinated mastery. I could not but acknowledge such undeniable ability, which I did in my own impulsive way, having a love for all young children which, coupled with my rather grudging admiration, sent me hot-foot to the young prodigy to give my public blessing on his major debut.

"I watched his career with desultory interest, but was gone before he had progressed very far."

He asked another question for Beethoven for which I do not yet have the answer, and then went on to put forward a question for Debussy: "How do you like Pierre Boulez's conducting 'Pelleas et Melisanda'?"

Debussy replied quite simply: "Je n'aurais pu le diriger mieux moi-même."

The reporter also wanted me to ask Franz Schubert if he had really failed to complete the B-Minor Symphony, and if not, where was the missing section?

Schubert replied: "Yes, I made sporadic attempts, but was unable to commit my thoughts to paper. It is now completed by me since my transition, and may possibly be transmitted to your world should conditions be suitable."

The question to Liszt was: "What happened to the manual of piano technique you wrote for the Geneva conservatoire? Please locate the score for us."

Liszt replied: "This massive tome I donated to my daughter, Cosima, to do with as she wished. I found it too cumbersome in weight and content for my own pupils, choosing rather to communicate verbally my own methods of teaching."

For Bach, the question referred to the art of fugue. It read: "Please give us your preferred instrumentation for the 'art of fugue'."

I am a little ill at ease with Bach and would hesitate to ask him any questions, but fortunately for me, Sir Donald Tovey came up with the answer. He said: "Bach when writing this illuminating work had not decided what combination of instruments could be used to the best effect. After his demise, he continued to consider the problem, and settled finally in favour of stringed instruments to classify the work into the chamber music category. The instruments should consist of two each of violin, viola and 'cello, combined with one double-bass. This would require a rearrangement of some sections by a skilled hand."

I asked Tovey why a double-bass should be included— it seemed out of place to me—and he replied it was necessary to provide a balance and to be the exponent of the 'figured bass'.

There was one other question addressed to Mozart, asking him to disentangle the exact order of his symphonies, giving key signatures, Köchel numbers as presently used, and stating if any of the symphonies presently thought to be his are, in fact, by other composers. He also asked for Mozart to explain his intended symbolism in the Magic Flute, and say who really wrote the libretto.

At this question I boggled. For one thing, Mozart is a very, very rare visitor to me, and for another it would take days or weeks to get a reply to the first part of the question. So, with apologies to the American news magazine, I would hesitate to attempt to ask Mozart those questions even if he became available for communication! It would be like demanding him to prepare a catalogue!

I have given some idea of my earlier life already in this book, but in the light of the constantly reiterated suggestions of my mysterious musical training, I think it worth explaining a little more about the sort of childhood I had, and the extent of my musical education.

I was born in Clapham, which was then beginning to lose its original middle-class respectability and was becoming poorer as the residents with a little more money gradually moved farther out of London.

When I was very small my father did not go out to work. I have never been able to understand why, because though we had an income from a hall at the back of our home which was let out for weddings, ballroom dancing, etc., the amount this brought was very meagre and fluctuating.

My mother would take over the catering for the various functions that were held in the assembly hall, and that way she made a little extra money. But it was a precarious living. When there were no bookings for the hall, there were added hardships. Occasionally the lettings did yield sufficient for us to have a few little extras, like a visit to the cinema, or a pantomime, but most of the time our family income was very inadequate and just met our basic needs.

My father was a healthy enough man, a year younger than my mother, and it seems strange to me now that he never took a job, though it may have been a period of unemployment for all I know. Children in those days were not told much about parental problems.

However, eventually the income from the hall became totally inadequate, and my father had to go out to work. He had been trained as an electrical engineer, and he went into that line and remained in it for the rest of his life. But that work was not particularly well paid in those days either.

There was, as you can imagine, neither the money nor even the inclination in my home to go to concerts or listen to classical music. In fact, I don't think that my parents would have bothered to attend musical functions even if they could have afforded it. The only musical connection at all was that my mother quite liked to play the piano and sing a little. But then she had been brought up in an entirely different environment from Balham. Her parents had been very 'well-to-do' once, and that period of affluence had lasted throughout her childhood. She started life waited on hand and foot, learning the social graces, and finished up as a drudge to our big house.

I can remember when I was small she would just occasionally play one or two pieces on the piano, but she had very little time for anything so relaxing. There was our rambling house to look after, three children and the running of the assembly hall. And when she began to get arthritis in her hands, her playing died out completely.

We did have a radio—not when I was a very small girl

—but my father bought one eventually. The radio, however, was not there for us children to use. It was my father's property and to touch it or try to tune it was forbidden. Even he didn't use it a great deal. There was no electricity in our house in those days, and the wireless had to be run on batteries which often needed recharging. This cost money, and therefore my father was a bit frugal about using the radio.

When it was switched on my parents' choice was programmes like variety concerts and comedy. Then, after my father died in 1944, my mother had the habit of listening to the Saturday Night Theatre Programmes. She would also tune into the Palm Court Orchestra and programmes of very light music. If any music was broadcast which was what she called 'heavy', she would promptly switch off. And I think I rather took my cue from her in this way.

Therefore I knew very little about classical music and my knowledge is still slight when it comes to the music the composers wrote while they were here. The number of concerts and recitals I have been to can easily be counted on the fingers of one hand, though perhaps this will be remedied when there is spare time and more money. And such musical events as I have attended have nearly all been very recent treats from friends since the 'psychic' music began to be known.

The first semi-classical music I ever heard was that played at the ballet classes which were held in our assembly hall on Saturday afternoons. My mother used to do the catering for these classes—she made lemonade from powder for the children, and cakes and biscuits, also cups of tea for the mums. She couldn't leave me in the house on my own—I suppose my brothers were always off somewhere on Saturday afternoons—so from the time

I could walk she would take me downstairs with her. While her attention was occupied serving and preparing food, I would creep off and get in on the ballet classes, carefully tucking myself at the back where I thought no-one would see me.

This embarrassed my mother who was a woman with a great deal of pride, and eventually she went to the teacher and said: "I really must pay for my daughter because she will keep joining in your classes."

The teacher said it really couldn't be helped as I had to be there to be looked after, and eventually they came to some sort of arrangement where my mother paid a nominal amount for my lessons.

That was the extent of the music I heard when I was very young, except for the jazzy stuff which they played for the ballroom dance classes which were also held in our assembly hall on Fridays. I didn't go to those, but the music would drift up through my bedroom window, and I learnt a lot of the latest dance tunes that way.

To return to the ballet music, it really wasn't very representative of anything that one might hear at Covent Garden. We danced to the sort of tumpty-tum music which is used for ballet exercises and which never seems to have much of a tune; only a definite beat. The only time when excerpts from the classics were used was once a year when the ballet teacher would put on a display of dancing for all the proud parents. And even then, the lighter type of pieces were used—not what I would call real classics. I remember pieces like "To A Wild Rose" and various bits of rather Victorian music which were quite pleasant to dance to, but not amongst the world's great classics.

The urge to learn the piano only came after Liszt had been to see me. Perhaps he put the idea into my head—I don't know. I started to pester my parents to be allowed to learn and my parents promised that if I passed a ballet examination they would try to afford the money. With this as a spur, I passed the exam, and the man who played for the ballroom dance classes was hired to teach me.

To tell the truth, I don't think he knew a great deal about music, but he taught me a few chords and how to vamp a bit. He had his problems, though, in that many notes on our piano didn't play, which was limiting for both of us. After a short time my parents decided they were wasting their money and my time, and they found me another music teacher who lived in a nearby road. He was obviously more qualified, and I had to go to his house near Tooting Bec Common for lessons, which at least meant I was learning on a piano that actually worked.

I enjoyed my piano lessons and never minded practising because I really wanted to learn. At home, apart from the dud keys, the only problem was that our piano was kept in what was called the 'sitting-room'—a room kept for the rare occasions when we had visitors.

As I mentioned, there was no electricity in the house and no heating except by coal fire and the sitting-room was lit only by two gas brackets. As my mother would never light a fire unless it was a very special occasion, I used to have to practise in this big, draughty, totally un-heated room. In the winter I can remember actually cry-ing because I wanted so much to practise, but my fingers were so cold and stiff that I could hardly move them, let alone play scales. It meant, of course, that I didn't prac-tise all that much even though I was so keen. And in any case, the piano lessons only lasted for a short while. Per-haps a year or so. There were so many financial ups and downs in our household that piano lessons would have been the first economy in any emergency.

But I went on trying to play a little on my own. In my teens I had two terms with a teacher who was an LRAM, and I paid for these out of my own money which I earned running errands. She was a good teacher and knew what she was about. She gave me a much better idea of music; taught me some music theory, and I learned more about keys and key signatures. She also taught me something about time signatures—though not the more complicated ones.

Alas, I promptly got rusty again when war broke out and lessons had to be dropped. There was a last series of piano lessons which lasted for just over one year after the war, from 1951 to 1952 when I was married.

That was my entire musical education up until then. My father was quite unmusical—he had a pleasant tenor voice (untrained) and sang to himself occasionally, but that was about it. I certainly wasn't being fed music from any other sources. There were no piano lessons at school, I had no friends who came from musical homes. Private tuition was available to those able to pay the fees for piano training. My mother was far too busy to let me keep bringing children home and she liked me to help her in the house so that I rarely got out. I used to get rather tired with the amount of housework that I had to do in addition to all the school homework. But that was the way things were done in those days.

My first encounter with classical music came while I was working in the Civil Service. There was a girl in the office where I worked who was a fanatic about opera, and I remember her going round and round trying to find someone who would go to Sadlers Wells with her one evening. She was a nice person and really, just to oblige her, as she didn't want to go alone, I said I would use the other ticket. It was a Mozart opera, 'Cosi Fan

Tutte'. And frankly I didn't think much of it. I decided that the opera was quite amusing, but not particularly impressive—not to me, anyway. I certainly didn't become an opera lover overnight. I couldn't for the life of me understand why the other girl was so very enthusiastic.

But I don't like *all* classical music even now. Poulenc has visited me once or twice and tried to give me some pieces, but honestly I didn't really care for the music he was giving me. Perhaps it is only that I don't understand it, but certainly I find the music not very attractive.

Nowadays we do have some classical music in the house as people have very kindly given us a few recordings and a small, cheap record player. I keep thinking that I ought to have a listening session, but unless it is a very short and interesting piece of music playing, I am inclined to get bored and restless. The trouble is I'm far too active to sit and listen.

And I most certainly cannot tell whose music is whose. Sometimes we switch on the radio and I'll say to my daughter: "That's Schubert. No, it's not. It's Mozart. Or could it be Beethoven?" And I'm generally wrong every time.

But then, sometimes, even very distinguished musicians can't tell. Hephzibah Menuhin once said I believe, that if you find some of the lesser known works of Haydn, Beethoven, Mozart and Schubert, even musicians can find it difficult to tell who wrote which pieces. And apparently you have to be quite an expert on Handel not to get him confused sometimes with Bach.

The point of my explaining all this is to try to make it clear that mine was not the sort of privileged childhood that goes with visits to concerts, and a general background of culture. In fact, altogether my life has been no bed of roses. Even school was difficult, though, without being

boastful, I was quite clever. And I am not being boastful
but just stating a fact, because Liszt has impressed on me
that if one has a clever brain it is God-given, and there is
nothing wrong in being grateful for one's talents. Anyway, I was clever and I won a scholarship to the local
Grammar School, and the authorities allotted a grant
towards my school uniform as my parents would not have
been able to buy it for me. There, I was always in a class
of girls older than myself and they were mostly paying
pupils—and sometimes snobs, too. Fortunately we all had
to wear uniform, so the state of my family's fortunes
wasn't so obvious as it might have been. But even so, there
were still hurtful moments. My clothes sometimes became
shabby and my shoes scuffed.

"Your shoes are awful," the more affluent girls would
say. "Why doesn't your mum get you a new pair?"

For me, in those days, a new pair of shoes would have
had much more meaning than tickets to a concert of
classical music. As it was, there was rarely the money to
spare for shoes and certainly none for concerts.

All this rather gloomy tale of woe is leading up to another point. One of the questions that I get asked very
frequently—usually by people who have been able to
bring themselves to accept that there is something super-
natural about my music—is "Why you?"

Why me, indeed! For many years I asked myself the
same question. Long before the music began to come to
me and right back to the days when I constantly saw
people from another plane without any idea of their purpose. And while asking, 'Why you?' people generally add:
"And why is it always famous people that you see?"

The answer to that is that I do not only see famous
people. I see ordinary people from Egyptian, Greek,
Roman and other times. I see people who have most

probably passed over quite recently, and even though they may give me their names, nine times out of ten those names mean nothing to me. Perhaps they might to some-one else I know, but not to me. It would be like basing a conversation on someone who perhaps I saw idly while travelling on a bus; someone totally unremarkable.

The answer to 'Why you?' is more involved, but Liszt has explained it to me. I asked him the same question—"Why me?" and he said: "Because you volunteered. Long before you were born."

I was startled at first, but thinking about what he said, I decided that if one can accept there is a life after death, why should there not be a life before birth?

Liszt said: "You agreed to be the link between us and the world when you were in another aspect of your life."

These are things that one can never hope to prove, but looking back it does seem as if my whole life has been pre-paring for what has been happening to me for the last few years, and that every twist and turn has been leading up to my being able to take down this music.

I asked Liszt why, if they planned for me to be the link and to do this work, they didn't let me be born into a family where I might have had a better musical training.

"You have sufficient training for our purposes," he said. "Had you been given a really full musical education it would have been no help to us at all. In the first place a full musical education would have made it much harder for you to prove that you could not be writing our music yourself. Secondly, a musical background would have caused you to acquire too many ideas and theories of your own. These would have been an impediment to us."

He also pointed out that a highly trained musician would probably be too preoccupied with a musical career to be willing to devote time to work with discarnate musicians.

I also said, perhaps a little crossly, that they might have eased my life a little if they had plans for me. I felt, I said, that it had been so hard that I had become crushed—which seemed likely to hinder the work.

"I know there are people who have suffered far more than me," I said to him, "but I do think I've had more than my fair share. Was that necessary?"

He looked at me with those very bright blue eyes of his and said: "Before you were born, and when you agreed to be our link, you also had to agree to a certain amount of suffering in order to be sensitised. Suffering, such as you have had, helps your type of powers to function. People who lead easy, placid lives are not sufficiently sensitised for communication with us to take place easily."

Perhaps I didn't look convinced, because he went on to say, quite gently: "Your life hasn't been easy. You suffer emotionally because it was intended that you should. It was also intended that you would learn to control your feelings of sorrow and rise above all that happens to you. And it is the ability and the willpower to do this which gives you that steadfastness that we need to work through you."

I thought about this a great deal after we had talked and I came to the conclusion that though I am naturally placid, all the things that have gone wrong in my life have added a sort of passivity—an acceptance of the worst that can happen. I rarely fight against things if they are only personal issues, and I suppose it is this passive strain in me that makes me a suitable medium.

I am not really sure whether or not I could be called emotional. I don't think so. I don't give way to emotions—like anger or impatience, and I don't cry easily. I've been through terrible tragedies and have always been able to keep my composure. I have been vulnerable, though, to people who say unkind things to me. I suspect that this may have something to do with the atmosphere in my home when I was a child. I remember my mother often told me she hadn't wanted me. I know now that she meant I was unplanned, and another burden at a time when she already had far too many, and I realise she loved me. But as a child I took her words literally and somehow I think it was perhaps that remark that was one of the things that had made me over-sensitive to any kind of rejection from another human being—but even the latter I am coming to accept without being concerned.

I also found it difficult to reconcile a kindly Lifeforce with little thalidamide babies and other suffering children, but Liszt explained that they had chosen to be born in this way because, perhaps, they needed the experience to learn patience or courage. He explained that we all need to learn different kinds of fortitude in our lifetime, and that to enter this world provides the opportunities to learn many things that cannot readily be learned in a state of trouble-free tranquillity.

"How," he said, "can you learn courage without facing danger? How can you learn to be cheerful without cause for sorrow? How can you learn compassion for others without suffering yourself? These are qualities of character which cannot be developed unless there is a challenge to face."

What he said was able to make me understand the reasons for my own disrupted and apparently disorganised life. But I am, I am afraid, human enough to hope that perhaps it will be a little more peaceful from now on. Liszt assures me that it will in some ways.

CHAPTER THREE

The Composer's Plan

"I am most intrigued with what has been happening in regard to your music as are many of the souls on this side who have been coming from time to time endeavouring to give to the world some of their new works.

"As a musician of sorts myself I am very happy indeed to be in effect the compere, if I can so call it, at this session. There are a crowd of souls gathered together, most of us musicians, and we are all most interested in what is transpiring, and we are all working together in a body in the hope that we can make some impact on that world of yours and bring some reality and truth into it.

"There is more in all this than perhaps meets the eye. In fact we know so, and I am sure you are aware of the fact yourself. It is not only music we are interested in, though music is our life. All of us here are very dedicated to music. We live in a world where music plays a very vital part indeed, and apart from coming through and endeavouring to use you as an instrument to give the world music of the soul, we are anxious to change if we can your world; change the thoughts of man. By the efforts of many souls here, we should be able to bring man to a greater realisation and understanding of the purpose of life."

That was Sir Henry Wood speaking to me through a

direct voice medium, Leslie Flint, and explaining again the purpose of the composers in giving me their music.

Sir Henry made that confirmation of the composers' plan in the summer of 1970, and by then the work was beginning to progress well.

But I suppose the fact that my music—I call it mine, though it is, of course, not the result of any creative skill on my part—is known today, really dates back to my mother's death.

If there is, as I believe, a pattern and a destiny in life, one of the important threads of mine began in 1961, which was probably one of the worst years of my life.

I had lost my husband in the August of that year, and in the previous January my mother died. My father had died long before and when I married in 1952, my husband and I had moved into one room in my mother's big house in Balham. The same house where I live today.

It was intended as a temporary measure. My husband and I had enjoyed the briefest courtship after being introduced by a friend who lived nearby and who, like both of us, was interested in Spiritualism and world religions. At that time I was working for the Civil Service, and it was my E.S.P. that had sent me delving into Spiritualism to see if it could explain any of the mystical things that had happened to me over the years.

My husband's name was Charles Philip Brown. He had been trained in horticulture and agriculture—his father had been Minister of Horticulture for the Department of Agriculture in Egypt under King Farouk. Charles had spent part of his life working as a journalist and was a specialist on Middle East affairs.

Charles's father, Sir Thomas William Brown, died in Egypt in September 1950, and Charles decided to return to Britain to live and work. Not long after his return, we met. He was a widower, and I wasn't exactly a teenager. We were immediately attracted to each other at our first meeting and he asked if I would go out to dinner with him.

I accepted, and that was the beginning of the sort of whirlwind courtship which I had never expected would happen to me.

I remember he took me to dinner at a restaurant in Baker Street—the West End of London. It was rather a smart place and seemed very expensive to me. I had hardly been anywhere at all, and the evening was a real treat. We arranged to meet again very soon—and then again, and soon decided we could be very happy together.

Five weeks after our first meeting we were married.

Charles was working as a freelance journalist by then, and it was a very insecure existence. We had a small amount of savings, and we intended to add to them and move into our own home as soon as possible. Already the house in Balham was beginning to show signs of decay that has now firmly taken over. There was no money for repairs, and we would have liked to have lived somewhere more pleasant—if we could have managed it.

We were never to move from that house. We had terrible ups and downs. For a week or two Charles would earn a lot of money, but that would all be swallowed up on the build-up of everyday bills. Then the work seemed to fall off completely. We simply could not make ends meet.

Nevertheless, we were very happy with each other. So much so that I can never imagine myself remarrying. He was very gentle and had a delightful kind of old-fashioned courtesy. He never so much as kissed me until *after* we were engaged. I loved him all the more for this reserve. It meant our relationship had a large element of companionship in it as well as love. And I think, looking back, that I had been very lonely for most of my life until we met.

We had a great deal in common. He was sympathetic and very interested in my E.S.P., though he never heard or saw himself.

He had been married once before—but spoke little of his first wife. It was a great tragedy to him when she died very young, and he told me that he had never expected to marry again. But she herself on her deathbed had told him that she knew he would remarry and have a family and find new happiness.

His mother had died when he was a very small child, but he remembered her clearly and with great love. He took me to see her grave in Tunbridge Wells, and I could see that even after all those years had passed, it was a poignant visit. He had one sister who died during the war. Her name was Georgina, and we named our own daughter after her. He had been very attached to his sister, and this was another very great loss. He also had two brothers in the world of spirit; one who died as a child from diphtheria, and another who died in the Forces, of whom I shall speak later in this chapter.

The greater part of his family was already in that world to which he himself was destined to go all too soon. I began to see all those 'dead' relatives of his—mother, father, sister, brothers, and even his first wife. They sent frequent messages to him, often filled with vital details of an evidential nature. He began to feel that he had not 'lost' them, but that they were merely unseen to him. Most amazing perhaps were the communications from his previous wife. I found her to be a very sweet-natured person, and not in the least jealous of the fact that we were now married; in fact, she said she was very grateful to me for caring for him and making his life happier. Surely this shows that she had a very real love for him, and not just a sense of possessiveness.

One night, when our two toddlers who had arrived on the scene by then had gone to sleep, I was sitting up with Charles who often slept poorly, and she appeared. She had with her a youngster of about seventeen whom she said was their son. My husband at once retorted:

"But we had no child."

She asked me to remind him of a miscarriage she had had—which he had momentarily forgotten. The baby, she said, had been sufficiently developed for it to enter the spirit world and grow up there. She added that she had named him 'Mark Anthony', and my husband almost shouted with laughter.

At first, I thought he was amused at the thought of an unborn babe growing to maturity in spirit, but then he explained the reason for his amusement. He said that he loathed the name, 'Mark Anthony', ever since he had had to learn the whole rôle at school. His former wife knew about this and often teased him, saying: "If we ever have a son, I shall call him Mark Anthony."

This was about the last name one would expect anybody to give their child; something which helped to deepen my husband's faith in my ability to receive messages of an evidential nature.

So my husband was the father, not of our two children only, but of a third previously conceived child. He adored our own two, and they adored him, and he must have been very sad at having to leave them here in this world—but I like to think that he must have been greatly consoled by the reunion with his family and his first wife and their own son, whom he could now see for the first time. He had worked out the age the boy would have been had he lived on in this world, and said he would have been about seventeen years old. Just the age that he looked to me.

He had had one remarkable experience himself during the 1939–1945 war. He had come to London to keep an appointment with the Ministry of Supply, but had arrived far too early. He decided to take a stroll in Hyde Park as it was a fine day, and sat for a short rest on a bench. Presently, he became aware of a middle-aged woman standing hesitantly nearby. At first, he thought she might want to sit down but was too shy or apprehensive to share a bench with a stranger. Then suddenly she spoke.

"Excuse me," she said, "you may think I'm mad, but I'm a medium, and I can see a young man beside you. He says his name is Thomas, but you called him 'Tommy', and that he is your brother. He passed over very recently."

She said all this quickly and rather nervously, no doubt expecting a rebuff—as mediums, however, genuine, are sadly given all too often.

But my husband's interest was roused since one of his brothers was named 'Thomas' and he did call him 'Tommy'. But as far as he knew, this brother was alive, stationed in Burma with the Royal Corps of Signals. He explained this to the lady, who then said:

"Oh, dear, I am so very sorry. But he is definitely over in spirit, and says that news of his death has not yet reached you."

Six months passed before word came through the Red Cross that Tommy had been taken prisoner by the Japanese and died in their hands. The time of his death was just over six months previously—which tallied with the time of my husband's encounter with the medium in the park.

Tommy became one of the most regular communicators

with my husband—through my E.S.P. We named our son Thomas in his memory.

My husband must have suffered a great deal mentally as well as physically, because he wanted to give the children and myself the best possible. He worried a lot at his inability through his continual illness, to bring home a good pay packet. My mother also wanted the best for the children and me—as a mother is wont to do—and she was inclined to blame Charles for our poverty. But who would wish to be ill and see his family go in want? Charles most certainly did not. When he was well enough to earn some money, he gave it all to us, refusing to take anything for himself. And he gave me two of the most precious things in my life—our lovely daughter and our fine son.

My mother's anxiety must have increased as Charles's health deteriorated—and we were often too hard up to pay her the rent for our room. She had so little herself; she, too, had been left penniless when my father died, and subsisted only on her widow's pension. After the war was over, she had let the ground floor to the Boy Scouts' Association at a nominal rent, on condition that they took on responsibility for the upkeep of their rented rooms, which included the assembly hall. Unfortunately, the small amount she received for this was swallowed up in rates. There was no margin for even the most necessary repairs to the premises.

I could not myself go out to work since I had to nurse my sick husband and look after our two little ones. We seemed trapped in poverty. The battle to make ends meet drove me to jumble sales to get clothes for the children and ourselves. We brushed our teeth with salt because we could not afford toothpaste; we stewed and restewed the same tealeaves to get a cup of tea. We learned all the stringent economies of paupers, selling what was saleable to get some money for a meal, and pawning all that could be pawned. I even tried, in desperation, to sell the old reconditioned piano that I had bought on hire-purchase not long before my marriage. I had given up playing when I was married—there was no time at all for that—and it didn't seem likely that I would resume. But now I can see what a good thing it was that I could get no-one to buy it, excepting one dealer who offered such a ridiculously low price that my husband would not hear of my accepting the offer.

A few months ago, my daughter said that she could remember that we seemed to live on potatoes. And it was true. Potatoes were about all we could afford. They were cheap—sometimes eight pounds for one shilling—and I would serve them in as many different ways as I could think up. I baked them in their jackets, I boiled them, I mashed them; I tried out every way it was possible to cook a potato. Sometimes I would buy an onion or two and make a potato-and-onion pie. Occasionally, we would have rice for a change, or gravy made with cubes or gravy-powder, and then we would soak bread in it to make a filling meal. I used to think sometimes: "If only I could afford a bar of chocolate for the children." But even that was out of the question. Things were that bad.

Towards the end of 1960, with Christmas approaching, I was trying to think how we could make it a happy festival for the children and my mother, and I remembered that I had some 'postwar credits' being held for me. I applied for their repayment, and as our circumstances were so straightened, I was allowed to draw them. We were able to buy a few little presents and some Christmas 'fare'. My husband was clever with his hands as well as his brain, and often made toys—a dolls' house and furniture, dolls' carrycot, and so on. I made stuffed animals and knitted teddybears and a rag-doll—and all these things we made out of bits of wood, scraps of material. But the dolls' house he had made had become broken—having been accidentally knocked over by my mother's cat—and by now Charles was too ill to make another.

I had got to know the lady who bought a house in our road, which had belonged to a close friend of mine who was an ardent Theosophist. This little Welsh lady, with a heart of kindness, told the Minister of her Church (a Baptist Church nearby) of our impoverished circumstances and my husband's illness. And I shall never forget the great kindness of this Minister—a true Christian—to us in our great need. He called on us, and asked each of the children what they would like for Christmas. Georgina, who mourned the loss of her dolls' house, said she would like another one. Thomas, who was barely four years old, was not so specific in his wishes. On Christmas Eve, the Minister himself arrived with a marvellous, large dolls' house filled with nice furniture, toys for Thomas also, and a hamper of food. I was very moved at such kindness—which was as great a happiness to us, if not more, as the actual gifts.

Altogether it turned out to be an enjoyable Christmas—apart from my husband's poor health. There was a Christmas pudding, and I was so pleased when my mother turned out to be the one who found the threepenny piece. I don't know what happened to this threepenny bit—it must have been one of the last small silver ones to be made. Perhaps my mother spent it—on sweets for her grandchildren of whom she was very fond.

This was, had I but known, to be the last Christmas, not only with my mother, but also with my husband. On the 29th December, my mother suddenly had a stroke in the evening. She had been out to tea with a sister-in-law who lived a few doors away, and came back full of happy chatter. One sad thing she mentioned—which came to my mind later—was the unexpected death from a heart attack of a man who had been a great chum of my 'dead' brother when they were at the local primary school together. She had heard this news at the tea-party, and it must have reminded her of her own greatly-mourned son whose death in his early teens had overshadowed all our lives. I wondered afterwards whether this news had triggered off emotions which had caused the stroke she had that evening. Yet she seemed so bright before she collapsed.

I left her for a few minutes to go upstairs to see how my husband was, and whether the children were asleep. Then, I came down again to make sure everything was locked up for the night—and I had a habit of seeing my mother to bed before retiring myself, as she was quite elderly by then, and rather crippled with arthritis, having to walk with the aid of a stick when she went outdoors.

It was very quiet downstairs. I looked for her, and found her lying on the floor in the scullery where she had gone to fill a hotwater bottle. She was still conscious, and managed to say: "I feel all sick and dizzy."

I made her as comfortable as I could, but she was slipping into unconsciousness. She complained that her head was beginning to hurt, and lapsed into a state of coma.

I hurried out and 'phoned for our doctor, and told him that I suspected a stroke. Having had First Aid training I thought I recognised various symptoms. He confirmed my fears, and arranged for her to be removed to hospital. I went with her in the ambulance, and stayed at the hospital until about one o'clock in the morning. By then, she had pulled out of the coma, and managed to speak a little. I assured her that I would be round first thing in the morning to see her, then went home—as the Sister advised. She told me that now that my mother had regained consciousness, she was out of immediate danger—and I had husband and children needing my attention at home. So, I walked home—a long, dark, lonely, sad walk—and did not sleep at all that night.

She lingered on for two-and-a-half weeks, and I even hoped at one time, when she seemed to be making good progress, that she would be with us for a few more years. But it was not to be. I visited her as often as I could, and it became obvious that she thought she might die. She had been interested in Spiritualism for many years, and knew that communication is sometimes possible with spirit.

Realising she might not be on earth much longer, she was desperately anxious to make sure we could keep in touch after she had gone.

She kept talking about a woman who lived not far away in Balham, whom I had met just once. This lady held a circle—a Spiritualist meeting—every night at half-past-seven and my mother had been a fairly regular attendant of the Over-Sixties group which this lady, Mrs. Hosgood, ran at a local Spiritualist church.

While she was in hospital and just before the end, she kept giving me Mrs. Hosgood's address over and over again, and saying: "Promise you'll go. Please promise me." She so kept on about it that I promised I would go, and only then did she seem to be satisfied.

I think it was in her mind that she might not be able to communicate with me directly; but perhaps through another channel, like a practised medium, she might be able to get through. Perhaps she thought I myself would be too saddened by her death to be calm enough for her to communicate direct with me.

I was not with her when she went. I had had to return home to my husband and children. But I knew she had left this world before the official notification came from the hospital. It was a Tuesday, about two o'clock in the morning. She had been in a coma at the hospital for three days, and I was sitting up with my husband who was having one of his bad nights.

Suddenly I saw her. She was coming across the room towards me. She was smiling, her hands outspread. "Look," she said. "Look! I have all my teeth again. And my hands—my hands are all right."

It was years since I had seen my mother really smile. Towards the end of her life all her teeth had decayed through lack of attention in the years when there had been no money for dentistry. She had been terribly self-conscious about her mouth. The few teeth she had left were blackened stumps. She was made embarrassed by this and in order to hide the state of her mouth, she rarely smiled, and when she did it was in a restrained fashion. Her hands, which had once been pretty and delicately formed, had been ruined by years of hard work, and in later years, by arthritis. Now, she was standing in front of me in the house where she had spent most of her life, and the marks of the years had rolled away from her. Her hair was golden and thick again. Her hands straight, and her teeth white like those of a young girl. She smiled again and said, her voice light and happy: "I'm going to see Eric, now." And she left me to see Eric, my brother, who had died when barely fifteen, as the result of an accident.

I knew then that she must have gone from this earth, but my sorrow was mitigated by seeing how all her pain and disabilities had just vanished. I could only be glad for her.

It was half-past-seven that January morning when a

policeman arrived to say that my mother had died at about five o'clock. I knew she had gone earlier, but it had not been discovered that she had passed over until the nurses went to turn her. Her body was then taken straight to the undertaker's little chapel where no-one was let in except the near relatives.

On the Saturday morning, there was a knock at the door. I went down and found Mrs. Hosgood on the doorstep: the woman my mother had been so insistent that I should contact.

She said: "Do you remember me?"

I said I did. I remembered her coming to see my mother just once.

"It was your mother who sent me," she said. Mrs. Hosgood was a clairvoyant and had already seen my mother's spirit. "She told me that she had asked you to come to my circle, but that you are hesitating because you think there might be a charge and you haven't two half-pennies to rub together."

She smiled to take the sting out of the words, and waited to see what I would say.

It was true. After my mother had gone I remembered the promise I had made, but I was afraid there might be some charge, and I honestly hadn't even sixpence to spare. I kept silent, and she nodded as if satisfied to find she had been correct and said: "Well, you can come if you want to. There's nothing to pay. In any case, there is no charge. We have a collection plate and if anyone likes to put a shilling in it towards the refreshments and heating—that's fine. But it's not expected."

I went about a month later when life had settled down a little, and became a regular at the circle. When I could, I did put something in the collection plate, because Mrs. Hosgood used to give us tea and refreshments. She'd lay on quite a spread in fact, and she did have to heat the room especially.

She was a great comfort to me at that time. A plump, tall, very dark-haired woman, she was married to an ambulance superintendent. They were both middle-aged, and had no children, but there was a very motherly quality about her. And she was very psychic.

My mother was in touch with me fairly frequently there, though she really did not need Mrs. Hosgood's help to get through to me. She comes to me quite often, and it comforts me to see her looking so radiantly happy in her new life.

I found the circle company—and even more so when my husband died after his long, painful illness in the August of that same year. And as time went on I got to know a lady in the circle called Mrs. Pendleton, from the Balham Spiritualists' Church. She did, and still does, a lot of work for the Church; she was its secretary and she also played the organ for the services.

She played quite well and could manage the old organ then, but there came the day, after I had been with the circle for about four years, when the church acquired a new electric organ. They could not get enough people to tackle the new organ and Mrs. Pendleton asked in the circle whether we knew anyone who could play and would be willing to do so for some of the church services. I said that I had played the piano in the past, but never an organ.

She said the church would be very grateful if I would give the organ a trial, so I agreed to see what I could do.

That was in February 1965—and I was by then receiving music from Liszt. Playing the organ became rather an ordeal. Even though I picked out the simplest hymns, I would make the most appalling mistakes as the congregation sang, with me wishing that the floor would open up and swallow me when some of the most discordant notes made me, and others no doubt, wince.

In the end, we fixed some of the stops to make the instrument less complicated, and I'd just play away with gritted teeth, hoping for the best, and ignoring the foot-pedals completely.

I was so abysmally bad at playing the instrument that I used to slip into church whenever I had a spare moment and practise in an effort to improve. It didn't seem to help a great deal. In fact, eventually I became so embarrassed by my lack of ability that I decided I must find someone else to play. Not only was there the torture of struggling through the services, making a fool of myself, but there were so many other duties involved as well. I had to choose the hymns, select the verses that would fit the hymn tunes, draw up a list of hymns for the chairman and fix the numbers on the board, ready for the service. As I tried to pick out the simplest tunes, we seemed to be singing the same hymns all the time, which was boring for all of us.

There were several services a week, and I found the whole thing was taking an enormous amount of time, which I simply couldn't spare, as well as being a rather nerve-racking business. Also, my work with Liszt was quietly accelerating, and I had a job and the children and the housework to cope with. I asked whether someone else could be found to play, and when there was, I felt I was free to give it up.

But to my surprise Liszt became quite concerned when I told him I was going to stop the organ work. I had expected him to be pleased as it would leave more time for working with him.

"Please," he said, "please do go on with it, I can assure you it is absolutely vital."

To tell you the truth I found his insistence rather puzzling. I couldn't see how playing the organ—rather badly —in a local church was going to help in any way with his music. But he was so determined that I decided that he obviously must have some very good reason, and reluctantly continued with the job.

Liszt knew exactly what he was doing. Had it not been for his anxiety to keep me playing for the church, I might still be playing his music for my own pleasure in my own home, without other people ever having had the chance to hear what he and the others are transmitting to me.

Though I did not know it, the new organ was another step in the plan that began with my mother's insistence on my meeting Mrs. Hosgood. And I began to realise this one Saturday afternoon when I had gone to the church to practise for the service the next morning.

I had picked on a time when a Miss Glady Smith was giving psychic interviews in one of the Church rooms. She was having an extremely quiet afternoon because not far away in Tooting, a very famous healer called Harry Edwards was holding a meeting in the Co-op Hall. Nearly everyone had gone to see him. As I recall, only one person had turned up for a psychic interview with Miss Smith, and she was left there on her own with nothing to do but wait and see if anyone else might still arrive. To pass the time, she came strolling into the church where I was quietly trying out one or two of Liszt's pieces on the organ to see what they sounded like.

As she came in, I half-stopped playing, hesitating, but she said quickly: "Do go on—" So I finished the piece.

"I liked that," she said. "It was very lovely. Who wrote it?"

I didn't quite know what to say, not knowing whether she would be sympathetic, so I thought for a moment and then said rather diffidently that it had been 'sort of inspired by spirit'.

She was a quick, birdlike little woman and she gave me a sharp look. "Don't you know who inspired it?" she asked. "Is it coming from one particular person?"

Her interest seemed genuine, and as she was a Spiritualist herself, I said, though still cautiously, that I believed it was.

"Who?" she said.

"Well, I believe it might be Liszt," I said, rather reluctantly.

She was immediately full of questions. How long had the music been coming? How much had I got? Was it only Liszt? Did it come by automatic writing? I answered her carefully, the habit of secrecy with strangers so ingrained that I was finding it difficult to bring myself to tell her anything at all.

Eventually she said very briskly: "Look, I know some people in Wimbledon who belong to the Church's Fellowship for Psychical and Spiritual Studies. They've been Spiritualists for eight years and they'd be terribly interested in what you're doing. Would you come and meet them?" And she added as a kind of bribe, had she known—"They have the most gorgeous grand piano that you could play your pieces on."

My own piano at home was a reconditioned one. And my ineptness on the organ made that not much fun to play either. The idea of listening to the composer's music on a grand piano was irresistible. I said I would go.

About a week later she took me off to meet Hilary Wontner and his wife Judith. Hilary Wontner is an accomplished actor who does quite a lot of TV and films, and his father was Arthur Wontner, the famous Shakespearian actor. Meeting them opened up a whole new world to me. There was the beautiful grand piano—a Broadwood with a lovely tone—as promised, and people who were really kind and interested, and who began to introduce me to everybody they thought might be of help.

There were other friends trying to help by then as well. Betty Francis, a lady who runs a healing and study centre in Acton with her husband, Karl Francis, was one.

Betty had been a close friend of mine for a long time, and I think she was the first to whom I actually played the music. At the time, she lived nearer to Balham and we saw more of each other, and I knew that I could rely on her to be discreet and not to ridicule me.

She is not a musician herself, but she said she thought the music sounded lovely and she, too, tried hard to help and get people interested in what I was doing. But even with Betty I was reserved at first. I said also to her that it was 'sort of inspired by spirit'. But my caution was superfluous with someone like her who seemed to have extraordinary flashes of intuition. Her reaction was exactly the same as Gladys Smith's. "Do you know who inspires you?" she asked.

"I think so," I said, still hoping that I need not say. I was aware that Liszt's name was a very famous one, and I was afraid that people, even other Spiritualists, might think that I was fooling myself in thinking that one so eminent as Liszt should communicate with me.

She gave me one penetrating look, said: "Is it Franz Liszt?"

I was so astounded by her naming the right composer straightaway that I heard myself feebly saying, 'Yes' even though I hadn't intended to tell anyone at all that it was Liszt.

But the cat was out of the bag then, and gradually other people within the Spiritualist movement got to know what was happening. I would even be invited to give small concerts in my local church and some of the members of the congregation who did know about music agreed that what I was playing was certainly in Liszt's style. I found this encouraging, because though I had no doubts myself, it was reassuring to get some endorsement from people with more musical knowledge than I myself had.

At that same period I was also going around and having the occasional sitting with mediums myself. I was still investigating Spiritualism and hoping through it to get some enlightenment about what happening to me. At that time Liszt had not yet explained *why* I had been chosen for the work, and the world seemed full of people who would have been far more suitable than I was.

One day, I had a sitting with a man called Harold Sharp, who is a very reputable medium. He goes into trance, and has a guide called Brother Peter who speaks through him. It is very beautiful teaching that comes from Brother Peter, who was actually a monk in this life, and when he came through at my sitting the first name he gave me was Beethoven.

"Beethoven is trying to work through you," he said, and went on to explain that Liszt was in charge of a group of musicians who would all come to give me music.

By then I was beginning to be aware that there were plans for a group. I had seen other musicians and received other music than that from Liszt. Beethoven had been one of those who had come to me, but I had not mentioned him to anyone at all. As far as anyone in or out of the Spiritualist movement knew at that time, I was working only with Liszt.

Almost immedltely after this I had another sitting with a fine medium called Bernard Rodin who has now gone to Canada. He also said that Beethoven was working with me, and he named several other composers whom, at that time, had not yet contacted me. Subsequently they all did.

And finally I met Mary Rogers, who is the wife of George Rogers the MP. She is a famous medium and wonderful healer in her own right, and is a woman of great charm and distinction. She is very, very psychic indeed.

We met a mutual friend's house where I had gone for tea and she immediately started telling me about the composers.

"I can see Rachmaninov with you," she said, very excited.

"Perhaps he is," I said, but doubtfully. I had not seen him myself at that time, and it was a long time after that before he 'registered' with me. She actually saw him some months before I did. She was right about that, and told me many other things all of which proved correct.

The communications from these various mediums and clairvoyants was at least giving me personal assurance that what I thought was happening to me was apparent to others as well. But it wasn't really helping in revealing the point of these endlessly flowing streams of music coming to me from the other side. Surely it wasn't intended just to please me and the small number of the people in the Spiritualist movement to whom I felt confident enough to play?

Liszt was beginning to be insistent that I must get the music to a wider audience—but how? I couldn't play the piano well enough to give important concerts. I knew no-one influential or famous. I had no access to anyone in the newspaper world, in television or radio. I could communicate with the astral plane and other 'higher' planes, but I had no idea how to communicate with the public.

My small amount of work with those in the Spiritualist movement was really preaching to the converted.

But the strange trail, beginning with my mother's death finally led to the solution. Her great wish to communicate with me after death made her beg me to see Mrs. Hosgood and join her home circle. This brought me in touch with Mrs. Pendleton who persuaded me to play for the church services. Then Liszt's request for me to continue to try to play the organ led, via Gladys Smith, to the Wontners. And it was eventually through them with their connections in the more sophisticated world which moved me on to the next stage.

The day came when they introduced me to Sir George Trevelyan, Bt., a brilliant man and a master of arts who also belonged to the Churches' Fellowship. He was impressed because he felt that what was happening to me was something quite new. I wasn't undergoing trance mediumship—my music was being transmitted to me in fullest consciousness. He listened to me playing and heard the music sympathetically. He was, he said, no musician himself, but asked if he could have some of the scores I had written down to show Mary Firth, a colleague of his who runs musical courses at the college for further education at Attingham Park, of which Sir George is warden.

During this first meeting with Sir George Trevelyan, as he was quietly asking me questions about the whole thing, I began to see the spirit of a man standing beside us. He told me he was Sir Donald Tovey, and I described the spirit to Sir George, saying that I believed it was Tovey. I must add that at that time to me the name of Tovey was one vaguely connected with music and that was all. I was under the impression he was a music-publisher, until I got to know him—and, of course, at that period had no idea what he looked like. Sir George confessed that he himself did not know what Tovey was like in appearance since he had never met him. Later, he checked with Mary Firth (whom I had not met then) and others, and the description of Tovey was found to be quite faithful.

Now, there are some people who glibly try to explain away all communication as the result of some kind of telepathy. It seems clearly ruled out in this instance, as it often is with the spirits I see. Sir George had no idea what Tovey looked like. Therefore I could not have been unconsciously drawing the picture from his mind.

However, after collecting some scores from me, Sir George gave Mrs. Firth sight of them. On July 16th, 1966 he wrote to me of Mrs. Firth's first reaction to the music. He said: "She is left with no doubt as to the inspiration."

She expressed so great an interest in the work I was doing, that I began to send her regularly copies of the music I was receiving, together with various items of information that were imparted by some of the composers from time to time.

Sir Donald Tovey began to figure more and more prominently in the communications, although he never dictated any music. I had learned from Sir George that Mary had been a pupil of Sir Donald's. Later, her husband, Dr. Firth, O.B.E. became very interested in these messages as he had known Sir Donald as well.

But Mrs. Firth's reaction to the music generally was very exciting to me. One sonata from Beethoven was, she said (quoting Sir George's letter to me) "tremendously Beethoven and up to his middle period composition". I did not know what middle period meant—though I know now that people tend to divide Beethoven's life into several composition periods. However, "tremendously Beethoven" was highly encouraging. Again (quoting Sir George) she commented on one Chopin piece, saying it was "lovely and absolutely him". He added in that letter that there were moments which they found deeply moving and stirring. It was a very joyful time. It seemed that the validity of the music had been definitely recognised.

Because she is not a Spiritualist, I would not suggest that Mrs. Firth accepts entirely all that I myself believe, but I do know she feels there is no rational explanation for what is happening to me. In one letter she said that certain pieces bore unmistakably the characteristics of each composer concerned. And then she and her husband, and many others sought an explanation.

Sir George and the Firths and a certain Major Mac-Manaway who had become interested, held discussions about the whole matter, and decided that whilst I was obliged to go out to work to provide for my children, the musical phenomenon was not being given an adequate chance to develop.

They then had the wonderful idea of setting up a fund and throwing it open to all those who wished to contribute. The intention was to replace my wages in the School Meals Service, so that I could devote more time to the music. I accepted gratefully, feeling that the composers would be glad for me to take the offer.

The fund was set up provisionally for two to five years, and then Dr. Firth announced in a letter which was published in the *Psychic News* that he and his wife were not convinced that the music emanated from the composers named, but that there seemed no rational explanation for it, and therefore the Trust—known as the Scott Trust—had been founded to enable a full investigation to be made.

I must confess that I was shocked to read the *Psychic News* the announcement that they were not convinced as I had been under the impression that they were. And very much so.

However, I realised that with musical reputations at stake—such as Mary's long and distingushed one—they had to be cautious regarding their public pronouncements as to their beliefs and conclusions.

The whole thing apparently still hung in the balance, and I felt none too happy with the feeling of being, as it were, placed under survey. But the Trust made it possible for me to concentrate far more fully on the work, and for that I shall always be grateful.

However, as the months passed, I developed a sense of being under an obligation which made me more and more ill-at-ease. Still I decided to fulfil the minimum period of two years' working in association with the Trust; this, I hoped, would provide Dr. Firth with some measure of data and satisfy both him and his co-trustee Sir George, that the Fund had been a worth-while gesture.

Before the Fund was opened, I had been working conscientiously with the composers for four years, carrying out the work as a sacred duty and never dreaming that it could or would ever bring any financial dues. And from 1966 onwards, after I had been put in touch with Mrs. Firth by Sir George, I had sent a constant stream of music and messages for two whole years prior to the founding of the Trust—sending simply as one friend to another since Mrs. Firth was so interested.

Alas! With an allowance (irrespective of the amount), I suppose it was inevitable for me to feel that the Trustees would be looking for or demanding results and expecting certain developments, however unconscious this might be on their part.

I no longer had to go out to work as well as cope with all the household chores connected with our large, dilapidated home. But I no longer felt as free whilst working in conjunction with the Trust, and my persistent uneasiness with the arrangement drove me eventually to resign whether I had other resources or not.

I sent in notice of my resignation in March 1970 to give good time for the winding up of the Trust by May— and at this time it had still not been decided whether the royalties on the music were rightfully mine. Nothing was certain regarding my future financial position.

However, that in no way detracts from my lasting appreciation for all help given, and my sincere gratitude towards all who contributed to the Fund.

All through this period—starting from January 1967— Liszt, Chopin and Beethoven were pushing me to try to get the music out to a wider public. Sir George and others wanted to hold back. I was being buffeted between opposing ideas, but it seemed obvious to me that the composers should decide what was to be done with the music they were transmitting. Beethoven, in fact, made it plain that if there was no move made towards spreading the knowledge, he regarded giving me his music as a waste of his effort.

Opportunities were beginning to arise towards the end of 1966 which the composers wished me to accept. One was the chance to meet a correspondent from one of the important daily newspapers, and the other to meet—both through Mrs. Wontner—Monica Sims of the B.B.C.

They were both pressing for an introduction so that they could interview me.

Mrs. Wontner suggested that I should write to Sir George and tell him of these two wonderful opportunities. To my amazement, I found that both he and Mrs. Firth were alarmed at the prospect of my seeing these two people. No doubt they feared that I would be exposed to adverse comments—which I was prepared to face for the composers' sakes. Also, they might have felt that I could be exploited by would-be profiteers. Their alarm seemed contagious, since Mrs. Wontner delayed the introductions. But Monica Sims, who was then on B.B.C. Woman's Hour, was to be transferred to the Children's Hour in the Autumn, and asked to let us meet before she lost the chance to put something about music into the Woman's Hour. And it was agreed. But I did not meet the correspondent until June 1968, when Sir George and Mrs. Firth had arranged to be present.

Monica did indeed produce a fine feature about the music which was broadcast on the 17th October, with a repeat in the following December. The first breaking of the ice had taken place, and the response by mail was really pleasing. Letters arrived from many different people. Some were from musicians, others from people interested in psychic matters, and I tried to answer them all.

It did not take me long to find out that most people forget to enclose a stamped envelope—and it is surprising how quickly all the pence grow into a substantial sum. There was to come a time when I had to give up answering the stampless ones unless they contained a real heartcry—and there was to come a time much later on when letters began to flow in by the hundred from all over the world. Then it became quite impossible to answer them all. This avalanche of correspondence consisted almost always of requests for various information. I wish I could respond to each and every one, and give answers to all the questions, but I hope that some of the most often repeated questions are being answered in this book.

At the end of the following year, this first broadcast by the B.B.C. stood in good stead to encourage to launching of a TV programme on the subject of music. It began with the Sutton Young Spiritualists' Church, asking me to give a small concert for them. They had heard how downhearted I was as a result of the many setbacks and disappointments I had had, and so they asked me to give a recital and talk about the way the music came into being.

They invited the local press to attend the gathering at their meeting place and we were very fortunate in having Catherine Sansom, then of the *Sutton Herald*, to attend. She gave me a very good, excellently worded, write-up in her newspaper, and drew the attention of Peter Dorling, of the B.B.C., to the music.

After that, things really began to happen. Before I knew where I was, the B.B.C. were preparing a programme on the music and after that many more journalists wanted interviews. A recording contract with Philips came up and Liszt was delighted that at last he and the others were beginning to get through to the world. People were talking about their music; speculating how it was coming about; asking questions and pondering.

The composers' plan was beginning to take effect.

CHAPTER FOUR

Liszt

Having explained the extraordinary chain of events that led to the composers' music becoming known to the world, I'd like to talk about Liszt who masterminded the whole operation.

It may sound strange but I can say quite truthfully that I feel Liszt to be a great friend. We talk about everything under the sun together. Serious things—like the purpose of life, and metaphysics. He doesn't call it metaphysics, but that is the term which could describe much of our conversations.

We don't talk a great deal about everyday things because he states that it is my responsibility to live my everyday life as I think best. Also, I wouldn't dream of bothering him with questions about ordinary things unless it would bear on some momentous decision I needed to make that might affect the life of someone else. Only then would I ask if he could give me advice, or if he had ever experienced a similar situation himself.

When he does give me advice it is done in a very kindly way. He is never autocratic; he will say 'this is only my opinion' and he always leaves me to make the final decision. There is no question at all of him trying to make my mind up for me, or dictate my actions. I wouldn't let anyone do that anyway!

I have asked for help for the children if they've been
ill and an earthly doctor not immediately available, and
he has managed to bring help from the other side by fetch-
ing a 'spirit' doctor who told me what to do or helped by
transmitting healing power through me.

There are certain snags in my work with composers
from the other side which would not apply to the same
type of relationship with people who are still bodily here
on earth.

For one thing there is no point in not talking aloud
about Liszt or the others thinking that they will be un-
aware of the remarks. The polite fictions people use are
no defence against discarnate beings. They are often able
to pick up and read our thoughts in the same way as tuning into a radio broadcast. Therefore it may be quite impossible to keep an opinion on any subject from the composers. Thoughts cannot be concealed from them when
they are present!

Sometimes I find myself quite absurdly dropping my
voice if I am saying something a little bit critical about
any of them—because not all of them are as easy to work
with as Liszt. It's rather a waste of time to whisper as they
seem to know perfectly well what I'm going to say before
I say it. There is one defence—to 'scramble' one's thinking and sometimes I make a conscious effort to 'jumble' my
thoughts in order to get a little privacy!

Mind-reading can be a two-edged sword. I remember
one day when Liszt was trying to help me practise some
music and he kept making me repeat one particular phrase
over and over again. I had been through it about twenty
times and was getting rather weary. Then he said: "Come
on. Try it again—", and banging away rather petulantly
at the keys I thought to myself: "Oh dear—he is a fusspot."

He immediately caught the thought and before I could apologise—he had completely disappeared. Nor did he reappear for about three weeks by which time I was getting quite concerned. I felt guilty, which was unnecessary as I hadn't meant to be rude; and anyway, 'fusspot' is almost a term of endearment. Hardly an insult.

When he did reappear he was very much on his dignity, and rather aloof, and we began work in a very cool atmosphere. We had been going along for some minutes and once more he was getting me to practise something over and over again when he suddenly stopped and said somewhat quizzically: "I suppose I'm being a fusspot."

I was glad he had brought the matter up. At least that gave me the opportunity to explain that I had not intended to be rude to him. I think it was an English term he hadn't heard. Liszt's English is very good, but there are blanks. He doesn't always seem to understand our slang and the more modern words. I think he had probably never heard 'fusspot' before and thought it meant something very discourteous.

Liszt is undoubtedly the most regular of my 'visitors'. I think he finds it easier to communicate than the rest of them and therefore can spend more time with me than most of the other composers.

Nowadays he rarely wears the priest's cassock in which he appeared the first time he came to see me when I was seven years old. He wears ordinary clothes—sometimes very up-to-date ones, not in the least Victorian looking. He would not look incongruous even in Chelsea. He often wears a cravat of his own period—but they are fashionable now. It's the same with his hair, which is always rather on the long side, just as it was in his lifetime. Fashion has caught up with him in that respect as well.

I'm pretty sure he appeared to me as the Abbé Liszt on

that first occasion because he knew that had he arrived as a handsome young man, I would never have realised who he was. The priest's cassock was to identify him when I was older. As it did. And he would only have worn a cassock once he was in his fifties and after he took orders.

In the normal way people do get younger looking when they leave this world because in that life there is no disease or decay. Age is really only a sort of decaying process, so after death the effect of the years on earth just disappears. Liszt says that people don't usually become instantaneously young, although when my mother went over and I saw her almost immediately she already seemed to be much younger. She was 81 when she died, and when I saw her spirit almost before her earthly body had stopped functioning, she looked about forty. That was pretty instantaneous, but my mother was aware of spirit life. She believed in life after death and perhaps had some idea of what to expect and so could adjust more rapidly.

If people's ideas are rather fixed, Liszt says they stay in the state they were on earth for a while and it takes some adjustment and thinking before they can revert to their younger, healthier selves.

We do talk quite a lot about modern life. Liszt has a very keen interest in everything that is going on in the world today, and he has often said that he wishes the facilities we have now had existed in his time. TV, Radio, tape recorders, stereo radiograms, and things like that would have been a boon to him and the other composers, and he is fascinated by the way these inventions have revolutionised communications. I think this is one reason why he has let himself become so involved in the various TV programmes and radio broadcasts I have been asked to do since the composers' music has become known.

Unfortunately Liszt and the others cannot always watch

our TV as it requires an attunement with our dimensions. In the same way that my density of vision of them varies, so apparently does their vision of us. They can't always see material things though they are aware of them. Sense them, is perhaps a better way of describing it. They need a special kind of tuning to move about in our world and see it, just as we need a special kind of attunement to get through to them.

All their powers seem to vary at different times. For example there are times when Liszt is dictating to me and I'll be uncertain what he means and ask him: "Have I written that correctly?"

He might then say: "Well, what exactly have you written?" and I realise he can't see the paper or the notes I've put down on it. Yet on other occasions he'll suddenly say: "Stop. You've put a sharp there and it should be a flat."

Maybe he can sometimes see material things. Or it may be that he picks up the wrongly written note from my thoughts. This sort of variation happens to me as well. Sometimes my clairvoyance will vanish for hours and days on end, and I have even wondered whether it will ever come back. At other times communication with the other side is so easy it is like talking to a friend sitting on the other side of the room. I live in hopes of one day being able to understand exactly what prevents communication from working clearly and of getting to know the factors which bring it about so that we can learn to switch it on and off rather like an electric light. Perhaps it will never be as simple as that. At the moment, contact depends entirely on waiting for someone to come through and I am never sure if anything will happen or not.

I have a feeling that those on the other side experience the same difficulties. When they 'go away'—that is, when

I don't see one or another of them for a long time and I ask one visitor the whereabouts of another, I often get a very ambiguous reply.

"Oh, he can't come now, but he will be back soon," they say. I wonder if perhaps they, too, can't always get through from their side and how much depends on me, the atmosphere, the surroundings? I have worked out that it does seem to be much easier for those of them who were extrovert characters when in this world to get across. And Liszt, of course, was probably by far and away the most extrovert, which could explain why communication does seem to be easier with him than anyone else.

I remember in 1969 when the existence of the music was just beginning to become known outside spiritualist circles, the B.B.C. Third programme approached me and asked if I would be willing for them to make a documentary film about the work. Quite honestly I was rather dubious. I knew I might encounter much scepticism, and I did not know the line that the B.B.C. might take. They could have set out to make the whole thing look ridiculous, and possibly have succeeded. As it happened, my fears were groundless. The subject was treated very fairly and with admirable courtesy.

At the time of the offer I asked Liszt what he thought and he had no doubt at all about accepting.

"You must go ahead," he said, "this is one thing we have all been waiting for, and it will be a step forward."

The programme was to some extent the kind of gruelling, third degree test, which has become all too familiar. There were endless questions which sometimes seemed to be the same, and neither prove nor disprove anything, and there was a psychologist in the programme named Professor Hansel. Now I am sure Professor Hansel is undoubtedly a brilliant man but unfortunately he does not appear to believe in E.S.P. at all and refused to concede its possibilities.

There were also people who do believe in E.S.P. on the programme, so I wasn't quite alone. And then they asked me to attempt something which I have been asked to do many times. Would I, could I, work with one of the composers while the B.B.C. were there? My heart did rather sink at the suggestion. As I have explained, there are days when there is no contact at all with the other side, and I never know whether communication will, in fact, take place.

"I'll try," I said, "but I can't guarantee anything. It is possible that absolutely nothing will happen. All I can do is make an attempt."

The B.B.C. were prepared to agree to this, and back to Balham we all went, Geoffrey Skelton and Daniel Snowman who were making the programme, along with a sound recording engineer and all his equipment, and we all got ourselves settled down in the room where I work. I supplied cups of tea for the officials and waited to see whether anything would happen.

It only was a matter of minutes before there was Liszt, as reliable as ever, looking very calm and composed and telling me in his rather Victorian, slightly pedantic manner he was willing to attempt communicate a new piece of music.

"Be sure you give me something spectacular," I said to him, and he just smiled in a knowing sort of way.

Until that time Liszt worked by letting me hear his music first, either in my head or through guiding my hands at the piano. This time he indicated he wanted me to write the music as he dictated to me. I was to write it straight on to a music MS although I was sitting at the piano.

First of all he gave me the key signature.

"There are six sharps," he said, "and the music will be 5-4 time in the right hand and 3-2 time in the left."

Very difficult. I turned around indignantly to see him looking quite pleased with himself and said to Geoffrey Skelton after explaining what the instructions had been: "I don't think that's very fair. Trying to put something as complicated as that across to me while you're here." I had never had such a tricky kind of music from him before. In the past most of the music, though sometimes difficult to play, had been very straightforward 3-4 or 4-4 timing. Nothing too involved.

"Now try," said Liszt soothingly. "Come on." And he looked so confident that he could do it that it gave me confidence. Well, I thought, here goes, and we were off. He first gave me four bars of the left hand, and then he began to give me the right hand. It all looked very disjointed. The top line seemed to ramble all over the place, there were funny looking chords, and he seemed to be throwing in accidentals all over the place.

After I'd written about twenty bars I was becoming worried. My difficulty is that I can't tell what music sounds like by looking at it and I thought: "What can it sound like? It all looks so funny. It can't make sense."

So I asked Liszt to wait a moment and said to Geoffrey Skelton, "Do you mind if I try to play this?"

He didn't mind, but I found it far too difficult for me to sight read. I couldn't play the 5-4 timing against the 3-2 and I was getting myself in a worse and worse muddle. I tried to work the timing out mathematically down the margin, but that wasn't helping much either. And then Geoffrey Skelton asked whether I minded if he tried to play it.

I didn't know it till then, but he is a good pianist. He

looked at the music for a few seconds and then played it without a great deal of effort. It sounded rather interesting to me, but when he finished there was a deadly hush. I was apprehensive that he was going to say he didn't think much of it. Then he turned around, very, very slowly and said: "Mrs. Brown, I think you've got something here."

At that, my heart leapt with relief! Thank heavens, I thought, it's all right. And I settled down to taking the rest of the piece from Liszt who was standing there looking amused to think that I had had qualms over his new piece of music. I was saying mentally to Liszt, "Why don't you give me something more spectacular?" He gave a wry smile and said: "I think you will find that this will impress the B.B.C. gentlemen more favourably than a composition in the nature of a Hungarian rhapsody or a brilliant concert piece."

The piece of music, which Liszt called "Grübelei", was soon completed and Geoffrey Skelton took it away to show a distinguished musicologist named Humphrey Searle, who is a Liszt expert. He was impressed with the piece, just as Liszt had predicted. Liszt had been clever enough to place just one musical clue in the piece which helped to demonstrate that it was a Liszt work. Humphrey Searle said it didn't resemble any actual piece of Liszt's but was something that could well have been written in the last fifteen years of his life when he was doing some experimentation with new ideas. The markings, which Liszt generally gives me in Italian, were apparently in character, though he had marked one in French—"avec tendresse"—which Mr. Searle said was also characteristic of Liszt.

The musical clue was one bar which apparently very much resembles a cadenza in a Liszt's Liebestraum. The two bars are not actually the same, but Humphrey Searle pointed out that there was a similarity of construction. In Grübelei his right-hand notes of the bar are placed an octave higher than in the Liebestraum, and in the Grübelei the passage is written in sharps and flats; but the notes are the same.

So, the experiment ended well. But I was really sticking my neck out that day. With witnesses there when you are working with someone they can't see you can't help feeling a bit of an idiot. And you feel an even bigger idiot if you are sitting there with no-one at all to work with because all communication has temporarily ceased. Either way, working with witnesses creates a situation in which it is very difficult to win. It naturally makes one tense and self-conscious and perhaps nervous. But for the B.B.C., it is evident that Liszt made a supreme effort and really surpassed himself. He rose to the occasion wonderfully. Some people say that Grübelei is one of the best pieces I have been given so far. It has now been performed several times on TV. Peter Katin, who is a very wonderful pianist, both in technique and interpretation, played it both on TV and on my first LP. I can now play it passably well after hours of practice under Liszt's tuition.

Unfortunately, I was asked to record it for that original B.B.C. 3 programme, which was rather a strain. There was no piano stool at the B.B.C. studio we used and the chair was too low for me. The action of the piano itself was very stiff, I had a frightful cold and altogether felt very unwell.

I was very nervous as well. I ran through the piece two or three times and I knew it just didn't sound right. But I couldn't manage the piano and in any case I had not been able to master the piece. I knew I ought to try it again, but my head was swimming and I just had to let the recording go as it was. Poor Liszt who must have wanted it to sound so much better, was there, trying to 'put my hands on', but I was so nervous and tense that he couldn't get through to me.

I told him how sorry I was not to have played better and he was very kind about it. He said it didn't matter and that we had achieved the main purpose of the work. He is delighted that his new music is being played and accepted—but not just to boost his own ego.

The reason for the whole strange phenomenon which puzzles so many people is to try to help us know for sure that there is another life and a purpose behind everything so that things are not as hopeless as they sometimes seem. Liszt feels that the first step is to make people just begin to think about an after-life. His theory is that while people refused to believe there is anything to come after we have finished with this world, everything will continue to seem meaningless, which may discourage us from putting our best efforts into our life here on earth.

It would, of course, be quite impossible for me to have any doubts of the reality of after-life. The so-called 'dead', seeming very alive except that one cannot touch them or embrace them, have been part of my life for as far back as I can remember. And it isn't only in my own home that they appear. Some of them accompany me, especially if I am going anywhere that is involved in any way with their music. It is probable that they like to keep an eye on things.

Some time ago I was at the home of Peter Dorling, a TV producer whom I met when the first TV documentary was being made about the music. He and his wife have become good friends of mine and Peter is genuinely interested in all the phenomena that happen to me. I think perhaps he does believe there is something, but that it needs clarifying.

Anyway, this particular day after tea he said to me: "Is there anybody here today?"

Liszt was—as usual. And Peter asked me if I thought I could draw him. I hadn't drawn for years and even at school hadn't had much in the way of training, but I said I'd try. They found me a pencil and paper and asked me to see what I could do.

"It will probably be frightful," I said. "And won't look like him at all."

Liszt was most amused by all this. He arranged himself in an armchair—he does appear to sit on our chairs! —draped his arms over the arms of the chair, looked towards the light, turned his head so that I would catch his profile. He is proud of his beautiful profile, though not in the way he may have been here. He says that beauty is something that is given by God and we should be grateful for it. Not big-headed about it.

He proved to be a very good sitter. He sat there, quite still, while I got to work. There was a cushion that came almost to the top of the back of the chair, and I was noting where his head was in relation to the chair and that it came above the top of the chair while his chin was nearly on a level with the top of the cushion. Spirits are not solid in the way that we are, though on some occasions they are so clear that I could almost mistake them for people here, but that is rather rare. I think it may be something to do with concentration of vision, but while I was drawing Liszt in that chair he was successfully blotting out all that was behind him.

The sketch wasn't very good, but it was recognisable. By some fluke I had caught his expression. He was looking rather pleased and happy with a far-away look in his eyes.

Afterwards Peter Dorling sat in the same chair and it

occurred to me that he must be taller than Liszt, because his head was higher above the back of the chair.

I couldn't resist asking him to stand up, and Liszt knowing perfectly well what was in my mind came and stood beside him. Then I could see that Peter Dorling was definitely taller than Liszt.

There are times when Liszt has a sense of fun. For example, sometimes he will begin to tell me a comic story, egged on by his contemporary Berlioz, until they are both laughing so much that I never do hear the end of the story. There was one about Berlioz and a pair of riding boots getting mislaid when he was staying at Liszt's Paris apartment, a disappearance which appeared to be tied up with a lady named Camille. The joke in the end was too good to share, and I never did solve the mystery of the boots or discover the connection with Camille. They drew me a mind picture of her and she was a slightly plump languourous looking lady with heavy eyelids and a great deal of thick, fair hair which she wore swept back over her right ear. She had a full mouth, and a rather high-pitched voice and giggle. Liszt said she had a very sweet nature.

There was also an occasion when he managed to startle Barry Krost, the young man who now looks after all my bookings for interviews, recitals, Television programmes, etc., and who deals with people who ask permission to record or publish the music. He and a gentleman named Jack Boyce, who at the time was working for Philip's Records, had met to talk about the recording 'Rosemary Brown's Music' which came out in May 1970. They had made all their decisions about what should be done and were just about to call it a day when the swivel chair in the room suddenly spun round and round and round. There was no-one that they could see anywhere near it, but apparently Liszt who had been observing their meeting was showing approval. I believe Barry and Jack were momentarily petrified!

I flew to Ireland in May of 1970 to appear on a Late Night Television show in Dublin, and was rather nervous about it as I knew that I would probably have to go through the usual inquisition. Liszt came too. And when I was anxiously searching for my boarding card which I seemed to have mislaid he said, rather resignedly: "You have put it in your pocket." And sure enough I had.

I'm probably making him sound a rather flippant sort of person, which he isn't at all. He has moods of deep thoughtfulness when he becomes very serious. He is emotional and is deeply touched if people are kind and appreciate his music. I have actually seen him in tears more than once because he was so moved over something. For example, the first time he realised that I had accepted him, really believing he was Liszt and agreeing to work with him, and appreciating that we were able to communicate with each other, he was so overwhelmed that tears of joy ran down his face.

I think he had been struggling for years to get the music through to me. All my life he had been working towards making some sort of impression and perhaps not getting much success. And even after he had made contact with me there was still the question of whether other people would accept the music he was writing through me. His joy when recognition began to come from other people was wonderful to see.

It is more on occasions of joy that he does weep. I don't think he and the others feel sorrow as poignantly as us because with their different sense of values, what seems terribly sad to us they may know to be a passing trouble.

And they accept that perhaps even a great sorrow may have some wonderful purpose.

I believe that Liszt felt neglected as a composer when he was here. He certainly had all the adoration he needed as a pianist, but as a composer I think he felt rather ignored. A lot of his soul went into his music. Not the rhapsodies, perhaps, but the quieter pieces he wrote. I think he was trying to express something spiritual and he longed to hear his music played in the churches at the end of his life. This rarely happened and I know he is sorry that he never managed to accomplish this ambition.

This spiritual aspect of his personality may not have been fully appreciated in his lifetime. He has a deep concern for everyone. He really cares about people and if anyone is suffering, he wants to help. That's another reason for his interest in all our modern forms of communication. He said to me once that in his time people suffered a great deal. Hundreds of people could starve to death or be the victims of a natural disaster, and people in other countries would have no idea that it was happening. But today with the newspapers, with TV and radio we know much more of what is going on in the world and we can take steps to ease the suffering.

He told me that he believes things are improving all the time in this world. Though there is still misunderstanding and trouble he says we are on the brink of what he calls 'a dawn of compassion' when people who perhaps do not bother very much about others will see that it is only common sense to look after those who are less fortunate. Any section of the community that suffers often brings a chain reaction to the rest.

He feels he lived in rather a dark time. A time when there was a great deal of narrowness of thinking. He doesn't try to justify his own life—and there are people who say he lived a rather permissive life. But he does feel that if he were alive today he wouldn't be so criticised for the way he lived; his habits and adventures would be less frowned upon as the public's outlook has broadened so much—perhaps too much, some may think.

I suppose Liszt suffered by the standards of the time when he was alive. He had many women friends, but I believe this could have been because he has a very warm and affectionate nature, and that women did almost literally throw themselves at him. He was very handsome. He was a famous pianist—probably the best pianist there has ever been. He was a well-known composer and an excellent teacher of music. Girls responded to his charm as they did to Rudolph Valentino's and, in our time, the Beatles. I think a lot of the time he was just trying to be kind and it was very quickly misinterpreted.

He is very kind to me often helping in little things like observing where I had put my ticket for the plane. And if I were romantic about any of the composers who visit me—which is impossible, anyway!—I think I could be as regards Liszt.

He is so very handsome and he has beautiful manners. He is graceful and dignified. And he is romantic in himself. He says such charming things and one can't help thinking: "Well, here's someone who knows the art of chivalry." I think people who have loved greatly may acquire a great facility for expressing love, beauty, poetry and romance.

There seems no doubt that he did have associations with women but he did not attempt to hide those aspects of his life. At least he was no hypocrite whereas other people were behaving in exactly the same way, but were being very secretive about it. Liszt was honest.

And in some ways he is very proper. The way he speaks

is rather old-fashioned and perhaps a bit long-winded by modern standards. I like it when he tries to use our modern idioms. It does not always succeed! Once when he came to see me and I'd been rather ill, he said: "I am glad to see that you are yards better."

I laughed and said: "You mean miles."

He thought about this for a moment and said: "What is the difference? And besides, I believe 'yards' to be a better word to use." He gave an involved explanation saying that he thought I was considerably better but not completely so; therefore he thought 'yards' more suitable than 'miles'! I suppose he had a point there.

I have been able to form a clear impression of Liszt because by now I seem to know him quite well. After all, for the past six years he has been very much a part of my life. I have probably spent more time in his company than anyone else's since my husband and mother died. My daughter, Georgina, has seen him several times—sometimes on her own, and sometimes with me. She completely accepts his presence, though now she is grown up her mind is too busy with everyday things to allow her to think of him very much.

I suppose we think of him as one of the family, which probably sounds presumptuous. But he is involved, at times, in our day to day lives. For example, I was having a guest for a meal one night, and though we are better off than we used to be, money still does not exactly flow in golden rivers through our home. So, I was shopping in a supermarket with my usual care for the pennies and looking for a small bunch of bananas to use as topping on a sweet.

There were masses to choose from and the first one I'd picked up was 2s. 9d. I thought: "There must be some cheaper than that—" and saw another smaller bunch which looked more likely. Just as I'd stretched out my hand to pick them up, I felt Liszt at my side, and he said: "No. No. Those are 1s. 11d."

The label was actually turned under and couldn't be seen, certainly not by me anyway. I turned them over, and there, sure as he'd said, was the price: 1s. 11d. I was astonished and thought very clearly, directing the words to him: "How did you know?"

"By what you might call a type of sensing," he said, adding, "There is another bunch over there which costs only 1s. 6d." And I took the bunch he indicated.

At the weekends, when I go to the supermarket, I go round and round, thinking about what I need, and popping a packet of suger, tea—all the usual things in the supermarket basket without attempting to add up the price. By the time I get to the cash desk I haven't any accurate idea at all of what the bill is going to be. I generally go in with about £2 in my purse which I hope will cover everything but there have been occasions when I did not have quite enough money and have had to return some of the items.

This doesn't happen when Liszt is with me. While I'm waiting in the queue to pay he announces the exact sum total. For example, "That will be £1 4s. 7d.", and so it is.

This has happened several times now and he is always absolutely accurate to the penny.

I asked him one day if he followed me around the whole time and added up as I went along.

"No. It is not like that," he said. "It is a system that we have. I note what you have taken and compute it by a kind of prophetic intuition."

That left me none the wiser. Obviously they have mental powers that are beyond our misunderstanding.

As an example of how involved Liszt has been in my

family life, let me tell you about the time when he helped my son Thomas with his homework. When Thomas was young he accepted everything Liszt said as gospel truth without thinking any more about it. The same applied to Georgina.

One evening Thomas was trying to do a maths problem and he said: "Mummy, what's one square, plus two square, plus three square, plus four square—"

He had just about said that much when Liszt who was with me said: "Three-hundred-and-eighty-five." Just like that.

"Liszt says it's 385," I said to my son.

"Oh, good," said Thomas and wrote it down. The next morning he handed in his book at school and when he came home that evening he said casually: "Oh, Liszt was right about that maths question. His answer was correct."

That in itself was remarkable enough, but even more remarkable was the fact that Thomas hadn't actually finished reading out the question. The problem went on to 10 square, but Liszt had given Thomas the correct answer before he was half-way through the question.

I myself don't know the reason for these things. I think it may be involved in some way with time consciousness —discarnate beings are perhaps able to see ahead. Liszt must have known what the complete question was before it was spoken.

They obviously can see into the future to some extent. One morning Liszt said to me in the middle of working on a new piece of music: "Be careful today. You are going to have three fires in the house."

And we did. The teacloth, hanging by the side of the stove caught fire, a lighted match fell into a rubbish bin and set fire to the contents, and much more dangerous, a pan of cooking fat set itself alight. I rather panicked about that, and didn't know quite what to do.

"Put the pan in the kitchen sink," Liszt said. And as I hesitated—thinking the handle would be hot—"Go on. Pick it up. It will not harm you."

The thing was flaring high and without his encouragement, I don't think I would have touched it. However, I grabbed the handle and put the whole burning mass into the sink and the flames immediately died away.

I sometimes think they do all these extraordinary, quite unimportant things like warning about fires, going shopping and helping in various ways to show they are aware of what is happening on our earth. It could also be a sort of practice in communication as well. There must be some point. After all, how can it matter to Liszt what my weekly shopping costs?

But it is this sort of small incident which makes me very much at ease with Liszt. Yet there are the times when I remember that he is a great person, and a famous name, and then it seems difficult for me to be on the same footing as him. This is not really a lack of ease, but being with him is obviously quite different from being with someone from my own time and place who shares the same background.

I feel great respect for him, but as well as this, there is a rapport between us. The respect is always there, but it doesn't overwhelm me and I feel I can talk freely to him about my own feelings without having any impression that I could be bothering him or boring him, or that the details of this life are too trivial for him.

And we do talk about all sorts of things. He and the other composers, for example, are quite intrigued with pop music. They think it is quite fun and good for young people, providing the music doesn't become depraved, and they are a little worried that some of it is going this way.

A lot of pop they say is not music. Just fun. And they do find it strange that so many adults can take it seriously. They like and admire quite a lot of modern music, but not all. Some, they say, is no more than noise. Not music at all. Some of it they regard as experimental work while the composers try to find new forms of expression. These are often phases which they'll drop after a while when they find the experiment doesn't express adequately what they are trying to say.

I was listening to the radio while Liszt was present not long ago, and some of this so-called modern music began. It gave me a good laugh and I asked Liszt what he thought of it.

He considered for a moment and then said: "It is a series of vaguely interesting but rather grotesque sounds. I suppose the result might be called intellectually clever, but it is not music in my opinion. It is not possible to manufacture music. It must come from some source of inspiration. There are composers who can compose direct from their intellect, but the results will be unsatisfactory unless there is some subtle quality of inspiration blended into the music."

And yet Bach is fascinated with modern rhythms, and he has said to me on one of the rare occasions when he took time from giving me music to speak—he is not very talkative, that he feels he was a little too mathematical in the tempi of his music.

He thinks now that he was advanced for his time in harmony during his period on earth, as well as in other aspects of his work, but he believes that he limited himself by the strictness of the tempi that he used.

And some of the other composers have the same feeling

about the music that was created during their lifetimes. They now feel that perhaps a certain amount of what they wrote was inclined to be rather clockwork.

People sometimes marvel that I talk about the composers, and in particular, Liszt, as though they are real. Of course, the answer is that they are real. Only in a different dimension, and I am fortunate to be someone with whom they can communicate. Liszt is a great favourite of mine because it is he who seemed to initiate the work and it is he who keeps it all going.

I love the music he gives me, though now he writes quieter pieces more than he did on earth. It pleases him and it pleases me that a great deal more attention is being paid to his music now. There is a revival of interest, with moves to print his lifetime's unpublished works. And there are the pieces he has given me. I have more from him than any other composer.

But as well as the music, Liszt has tried to give me a glimpse into what lies ahead for us after death. I have asked him questions about God, the Universe and Death —the 'what's it all about' questions that have always been great mysteries to those of us on earth.

Liszt is a deeply religious man and very devout. He has told me as much as he can and has brought others to help explain. Much of what I have been told is beyond my comprehension, even though some of the things I have learnt have opened new doors and completely changed my thinking. But I will try to explain all of that later.

For now I would like to tell one more story which I think illustrates how kind and thoughtful Liszt can be.

It happened when three German journalists and one Hungarian photographer working for the magazine *Der Speigel* came to see me in the early part of 1970. They were at my home for about an hour and a half, asking questions and taking photographs.

Eventually the inevitable question came up: "Can you see anyone now?"

Well, I could. And I told them I could see my own mother and Liszt. There was a slight silence while they looked uneasily around the room as I have found people sometimes do, and then one of them—the Hungarian, whose name is Tom Blau—said: "May I please ask Liszt a question?"

I don't normally like to bother the composers with endless questions but this man had asked so nicely that I said: "Go ahead. I don't know whether I'll get an answer, but do ask."

So, he asked something in very rapid Hungarian. I looked at Liszt who said: "Would you please ask the gentleman to repeat his question more slowly. I fear that my Hungarian is not very good." For although Liszt is half-Hungarian, German is his natural language, with French a runner-up.

I explained all this to Mr. Blau who suggested that he might ask the question in German. Now I know Liszt's German is sound, so I said that I thought that would be a good idea.

Then he asked the question in German—which I couldn't follow either as I don't know German except for about half-dozen simple words like yes, no, please, etc. I looked at Liszt, who nodded and said: "Ja."

"He says 'Ja'," I said to the Hungarian, wondering what Liszt was saying 'Ja' to.

Then Liszt said: "I am going to fetch someone." And he disappeared. He was back in seconds with a woman who was also in spirit. I was able to see this lady very clearly indeed and I described her appearance, her features, face, hair, colouring and clothes. She had, I remember, remarkably dainty feet and she wore a shawl which she kept folding across herself and holding with her hands on her opposite shoulders.

Listz said: "Tell the gentleman about the shawl," and all the while Mr. Blau was nodding as I spoke, and he said: "Yes, she used to hold her shawl like that."

When I mentioned the small, dainty feet, he said: "That's very good. It is my mother you are describing." And he went on to explain how he had always felt sorry that he had not been with her when she died. "Now I feel better about it," he said. "I cannot thank you enough."

It seemed that he had asked if Liszt could bring his mother, and, as usual, Liszt had been helpful. That seemed to clinch things with the journalists as I had never seen Mr. Blau before, of course. It was just like Liszt to do something impressive at the vital moment, and this is why I trust him and value his friendship so greatly.

CHAPTER FIVE

Life after Death

When I was in my teens there were several long periods when I was very ill indeed. One after the other, I had acute anemia, a bout of rheumatic fever, and eventually the worst of all, polio. There were times when our family doctor and others thought the chances of my living very slight.

On occasions through those illnesses I think I was hovering on the threshold and I could see into another world. The life-after-death world that awaits us all.

Those who are in spirit, including of course, Liszt and the others who visit me, live on a different level of consciousness to us. It is not possible to locate their 'space' geographically, nor do they need ground to walk on, air to breathe or food to eat. But they do have scenery. On the other side there are mountains, woods, rivers, trees and flowers. But it is dissimilar from our world. More beautiful than we can begin to imagine.

I experienced the fantastic beauty of this different region at that time when I was so near to death. There were beds of flowers as far as the eye could see, massed in different shades and colours which lived and glowed. It sounds, I know, as if I am talking about fairyland, but that other place makes the most beautiful things our world can offer as no more than a poor reflection of perfection.

There are, for example, colours that we don't have here on earth. I have tried many times to describe them, But it is impossible—like trying to explain colour to a blind man. Some of their colours are much more vivid than ours; others are softer, but however I try to explain them the exact description always eludes me.

Throughout my teens I was always seeing this beautiful other world; travelling over hills and through valleys and wandering in gardens. I used to fall asleep without any trouble at all no matter how ill I was. My difficulty was always to wake up.

Occasionally I would see the same visions when I was wide awake. I could even smell the flowers, the whole experience was so vivid, and there are times even now when I can still catch those exquisite scents. But above all in both sleeping and waking moments in that other place, there was a deep, deep feeling of peace.

Having glimpsed that other world, I look forward to the prospect of living there after I have passed through death's door.

I have been able to ask Liszt all sorts of questions about his world and he always tries to answer so that I can understand. For example, I wanted to know *how* he and the others actually travelled. He explained by using a modern, science fiction word—teleportation. He said that he can travel about our world, not so much by thinking of the place where he wants to be, but more by thinking of the person he wants to visit.

He and the others who visit me think of me, and in that way get on to my wave length. By doing this they can 'teleport' themselves to wherever I am. It doesn't matter if I am in an aeroplane, in my own home, or, an unlikely eventuality, down in a submarine. It is the person, not the place that they use as a focal point.

I have also asked him the question which seems to many people the eternal mystery. Is there a God?

"There is, indeed," he said, "but not a God as those on earth think of Him. God is spirit. A life-force which permeates everything and is everywhere. Yet it is spirit which is aware, so that if people do pray together, the prayers register."

Prayer, it seems, works in a similar way to the 'teleportation' which spirits use for earthly contact. If we think of what is good, we should be able to get on to that wave length.

He explained that this Spirit is personal and yet impersonal at the same time, and is therefore something beyond our imagination to grasp because it does care for every life and does work towards good.

For example, he explained how in everyday matters our bodies, when ill or injured, will always try to right themselves—to heal themselves. This is done by the Life Force which is working all the time to try to adjust, balance and compensate.

"We could." Liszt says, "heal ourselves of most illnesses if we would give this Force a chance," but he added regretfully that we have not learned how to harness it for our own good.

It was while we were having this discussion that I put forward the viewpoint that it seemed unfair that we don't get the opportunity to know more about God. Millions of people never have the chance, or the intellect to think properly about Him. We don't have enough training, and we all need at least a modicum of education to begin to think clearly about spiritual things. There are still people who are almost untouched by civilisation and seem to have little chance to get to know or understand anything about God, even as we see Him—although perhaps their souls are close to God.

Somehow it seems unfair, and I said as much to Liszt, adding, though it must have sounded irreverent, that God could perhaps have arranged things so that we knew a little more; so that we could be *certain* He exists.

It was probably a stupid idea. How can we judge from our own viewpoints when we know so little?

But Liszt had an inspiring answer.

He said: "Perhaps I can explain most simply by an allegory. If you plant a seed in the earth it cannot see where it is going. It is in darkness. It does not know where the light is, or where the air is. But in that seed is the God implanted instinct which will cause it to grow and push its way upwards to the light and the air.

"It is the same with the human soul. The soul may be in darkness, but there is within it that divine instinct; an instinct that will lead eventually towards light and understanding. The soul will attain God-consciousness ultimately—though not necessarily during its life on earth."

He said, rather sadly, that while we are on this earth many live believing this is the only life, without realising that we can go on unfolding spiritually after this life here is ended.

I remarked that because of the usual Christian beliefs there are people who believe that one has to be 'saved' here on earth.

"That is not true," he said. "Life on your earth is rather like a nursery school. When people die and it appears that they have lived wasted lives, they still have the chance to go on and to catch up.

"Our purpose, working with you, is an attempt to make

people realise this, and therefore give hope. Your lives on earth could become happier if people knew that it is only a preliminary to the wonderful life after death."

Hell, Liszt says, is a self-made thing.

"If people have lived lives that have been deliberately destructive, or by wilful neglect or action caused suffering to others, when they arrive here on our plane, then they have to face what they have done.

"Their conscience can no longer be stifled because there is nothing between them and their conscience as there is on earth."

He explained how on earth people can refuse to listen to conscience, but in the other world, it is impossible to shut out these thoughts and of course this can be a sort of hell. People do then eventually become very regretful and wish they had behaved differently. But providing this feeling acts as a spur for them to try to overcome their past failings, make good and compensate the people to whom have they caused harm—then the regrets can bring eventual happiness.

One of the most marvellous things that Liszt has told me is that when we die and we leave this life for our new home, we are always met on the other side so that we will not be alone and afraid. Usually some of our own dear relatives and close friends are there waiting to greet us and to show us around until we have settled down and understand where we are and feel at home.

I think this is wonderful. After all, many of us are afraid of going into what we think of as 'the great unknown', but once we know and can believe that every single one of us is met by familiar and loving faces, that fear can fade.

Those on the other side often seem to have foreknowledge of accidents, and can organise accordingly so that people are still met no matter how precipitously they leave this world for the other.

This would seem to give the impression that our lives are predetermined, and that the fatalists are right.

Yet Liszt says this is not correct.

He says that we volunteer for our life on this earth, and that before we are born we are given a sort of plan of what our life is likely to be. But it can never be quite determined how we will react to various situations or whether we will follow our appointed course, and therefore our actions can change our lives.

For example, when the music began to come through Liszt warned me that the work would mean a great deal of suffering for me—from ridicule, from jealousy, and from harsh scepticism. He said that people would try to exploit me, people would try to suppress the music, people would try to take command, and that people would belittle me. All sorts of hurtful things would happen.

He was quite correct. All these things happened to me, but he also said that if I would go through with it, what I was doing could be of value to the world. And for that reason I agreed to undertake the work.

But he did warn me, and I did have the choice. There have been times when I have suffered bitterly, and I have sometimes wondered whether I would still have gone ahead if I'd known just how much disparagement and even denigration there would be. Yet I know that really nothing would have stopped me, because right from the beginning I caught Liszt's enthusiasm. He has a deep sense of mission, which has become implanted in me. I feel that I am privileged to have been chosen for the work—even if it does at times cause me much heartache.

The point though about life on earth is that if we try we can get to a certain level of evolution where we learn to control our own actions instead of merely reacting to circumstances. We become more poised and this is turn creates greater conditions of calm in our lives.

It is necessary to practise thought control before this peace can become established, but I am convinced that if you do try to live a life that is centred on higher things (on God, if you like, for I can't think of a better word to use) you find protection and guidance.

This does not mean that life will be smoothed out for us, but we will be able to cope with it more easily and find that with constancy strength comes. I believe that as we sow, so we reap. If we keep thinking negative thoughts, maybe always expecting the worst, we will have negative things coming back to us. I know it is far from easy to keep one's thoughts along positive lines all the time; we just have to keep practising until it becomes a matter of habit that is so automatic we don't think about it. I'm fortunate that I have help from Liszt and the others, but even so it needs ceaseless effort to work towards being positive and to prevent frequent slipping into a negative attitude.

This life is preparation for the other life to come, but not quite in the way the Western churches preach. And I have asked Liszt questions about the first plane that awaits us beyond this one.

There is, he says, substance of a sort there. To each other those who dwell there are comparatively solid as we are to each other when on earth. But after death there are various spheres and levels of consciousness, and Liszt says that people gravitate to these different levels of consciousness and that some very evolved levels are formless where souls no longer need to assume any outer shape.

I asked him how people recognised each other if there is nothing to be seen?

"There is a sort of soul-sensing," he said, "when one soul close to another recognises it by sensing its presence and can identify the individual's atmosphere.

"This comes after a very long time," he went on. "It can take many years. So there is no question of suddenly being flung from one state of consciousness to another so totally foreign that the soul would feel ill at ease and out of its element."

"You arrive at this advanced state of consciousness when you really wish to, and are then in a state of bliss."

This intangible state is perhaps hard to understand completely, but might compare with "Nirvana" or "Samadhi".

Liszt explained that this last stage is a state of celestial consciousness where the soul is not interested in appearance but in *being*.

"Souls there have lost all insistence on personal embodiment," he said, "feeling that an outer form is no longer necessary. We only require our outer selves on the less subtle and less fine levels of consciousness where definite, visible form is essential."

I thought about this for a long time, and then on another occasion when he came, during an interval between working on music, I asked him how this fitted in with some people's theories of reincarnation.

"Reincarnation as usually understood does not really happen," he said. "The truth is subtly different from the teachings of a reincarnationist on earth.

"What happens is rather like the putting out of a fresh shoot on a tree or a plant. On earth, you think of yourselves as complete beings. But actually only part of you has manifested through the physical body and brain. The rest is still in spirit but is linked and one with you.

"The human being can be compared with an iceberg. Very often there is only a fraction of the true soul which manages to show through and express itself.

"This is one of the things that we who have gone before want to help you to develop and understand so that people while they live on earth can manifest more fully and express themselves to greater degrees."

He then explained to me how the same person never returns to this earth twice, and went into enormous detail to explain why it couldn't be. For example, if it were me, Rosemary Brown, who was supposed to be reborn, I would have different parents, different ancestry, different brain, body—everything would be different.

But part of me could be 'inserted'—perhaps 'infused' is a better word—into a new being.

When the physical body ceases to function at what we call death, that essential quality that was infused goes back to the original whole. So there is reincarnation in a sense, but it is not a repetition of the same person; generally when we speak of reincarnation we seem to think of exactly the same person being reborn again.

Perhaps we oversimplify the idea of reincaration. There is no common rule. We do not according to Liszt keep shuffling backwards and forwards between two worlds endlessly as some orientalist teachers claim. We may only come a few times. Perhaps only once. There is, Liszt says, an enormous amount of variation and no fixed principle at all.

"All incarnations are absolutely voluntary," he said. "Nobody is thrust into the world against his will. No-one has to go there. And this makes for justice."

He explained that we come back to earth of our own free will; perhaps to learn some new lesson. But once we are here, we have forgotten the reason for our coming.

And only a part has come through—the soul part that has volunteered to come.

For example, if on earth a man had actively disliked women, or suffered from some form of colour prejudice or racial prejudice, part of his soul's reappearance in the world on another occasion could be in the form of whatever or whoever it was he had felt prejudice against whilst on this earth.

Therefore the racist might return as a coloured person, the misogynist as a woman, the religious bigot as a member of a religious community which he had opposed. And in this way the lesson that all men are equal in the sight of God would be learnt.

Liszt also explained to me how we are not really a unit at all. Each person is soul with many aspects, and one day he expressed it to me in scientific terms.

"Think of an atom," he said. "It is made of protons and neutrons which all go to make up the nucleus surrounded by electrons. That is what a soul is like. These separate parts are held together in the nucleus, but the parts can be isolated. And it is the isolated parts of the nucleus of the soul so to speak which can manifest as various personalties in your world.

"These are what the reincarnationalist calls different incarnations—but they all belong to one soul which can choose which particular part of the soul it wishes to manifest.

"Let me try to put it very simply for you," he said. "Supposing we have a soul that has had a link with Egypt, and then put out another branch, as it were to perhaps Greece. That soul could then appear as an Egyptian or a Greek.

"It is rather similar to having a wardrobe of clothes and deciding which ones to wear; or like an actor who plays different parts. The actor remains the same. It is only the playing of the rôle on stage which makes him seem different. His own private life goes on."

Liszt seems very anxious that we should try to understand this slightly different angle on incarnation, or reincarnation. And I think now that I do understand better, it does seem more logical to me.

This is the great problem, though, to understand what those from the other side are trying to communicate. Something else I rarely speak about, again for fear of ridicule, is that Einstein occasionally comes to see me. He speaks—and very quickly—about things which are often far beyond me, and yet he is enormously patient and kind. I have noticed that as he speaks he has a trick of rubbing his moustache with his fingers in a thoughtful kind of way, and he has a habit of speaking as if he is just talking—not talking *to* me, rather as if he is giving a lecture to a class or even thinking aloud.

I cannot think he is coming to see me for friendly visits. I believe he is trying to give ideas to us, in the way that the composers are putting over their music. What he has to say is abstract thought which has to mature slowly in the mind. The ideas are so tremendous that he has a problem of expressing them in words, particularly as he is talking about things for which we do not have everyday terms. And some of what he says is so abstract that it is difficult to understand.

There are times when I almost feel that I do understand what he means—but how can I convey the ideas to other people so that they will understand, too?

It is like a flash of insight; for a short while I feel I have grasped his meaning—but then it has gone again.

I'm hoping that what he has to say will gradually be

assimilated by me so that I can express his ideas satisfactorily. But somehow we don't seem to have the language for it as yet.

Einstein himself has to try to talk in my terms before I can understand at all. He will try to explain in various ways, but I still don't really grasp it. He is always telling me that I must develop my mechanics of thinking, and I am hopeful that this is something that will come, too.

I first saw him about three years ago, but I can't place the exact time. There is a kind of linking between these people who come to see me. For instance, Liszt is an extremely clever, intelligent person, not only interested in music, but in physics and many things. I suppose that was how he got drawn into meeting Einstein. On the other side, people are drawn together by common interests, just as in life, and it doesn't matter which period of time they come from. Liszt often acts as a go-between for me. It was he who first brought Einstein to see me.

Einstein will say things like 'The time and space concepts of humanity will change', and then if I strain too hard to hear and to understand the communication goes. He also said to me once that we have a divided consciousness which will evolve into an amalgamated consciousness that will enable us to extract a true assessment of human values. I wrote that down immediately so that I could puzzle over it at leisure.

One of the things I like about Einstein is that he is very fond of children. He once said to me that he would like very much to work with children.

"They have a fresh intelligence," he said, "which is untrammelled by modern systems of education, which are inclined to stifle the individual's thinking. Present day systems of education aim at inserting quantities of information into the growing mind without allowing adequate time for assimilation and consideration of the facts introduced."

He sounded quite cross about it, but then one of his chief interests is education, and he believes this is where the future of mankind lies. Also he seems to have a pretty poor view of our intelligence here on earth. He once said to me that there were only ten people alive who really knew how to think, and how to use the thought processes that are available to those of normal intelligence.

Some time afterwards, when Lord Russell died, he then said that there were now only nine thinkers left. He will not tell me who they are—perhaps just as well.

Very diffidently, I asked him about space once. He rubbed his fingers over his moustache and said: "In a sense everything is in one place. And in another sense space is endless. It is one of those apparent contradictions."

He went on to add that once we understood the nature of space, space travel would become much easier for us. It sounds so difficult to fathom and I spend ages thinking about it without being any wiser at the end. I can only wait now to see what develops. I sometimes wish that a tape recorder could pick up their voices in the same way that I can. Then, instead of trying to write down the more involved and complicated things that people like Einstein say I could record them exactly and give them to people who are wise to work out.

However, sometimes I do try to write down everything he says by hand. This is a fairly laborious process, particularly when communication is not good, and with Einstein I do find it is inclined to fade rather a lot.

He did, on one occasion in the summer of 1967, give me an equation, which he explained was, in fact, 60 variable equations in two groups of thirty each, one group decreasing and one group increasing.

The actual equation was: $S(Q)R = $ Infinity.

$S = $ Sequence.

$Q = $ Quantity.

$R = $ Ratio.

What follows is from his dictation.

"S can be taken to represent the passage of time (history); Q to represent the manifestation of the Life-force (creation); R to represent the variable factors (conditioning of creation).

"S is passing through Q; that is to say, time is passing through creation subject to fluctuations of the energy quotient which operates in rhythmic frequencies as a great pulse animating life throughout the entire universe.

"The invidious question of the resultant domination over the course of evolution by a primordial originating impulse can only be discussed in full when all the secondary factors are taken into consideration. No facet of Nature can be separated from the primal impulse which set in motion endless chain reactions. These reactions may at times be controlled or interrupted or even halted; certain processes can be repeated, reversed or occasionally revoked. These are matters requiring profound thought and thorough research."

At this point the contact with Einstein faded, and Sir Donald Tovey took over the dictation, on the same lines of reasoning, and I think it worth repeating what he said here for other and wiser minds than mine to puzzle over.

"There are not, as it would appear, two creative aspects, viz., male and female, but one only, the creative energy-force which divides and sub-divides to produce numerous forms and formations of matter. Any manifestation in form or sound is an eruption of the energy-force from its pure monotype into a broken pattern. The life—or energy-force—is single, whole, formless, soundless and more powerful than all its combined manifestations, and is the only absolutely complete life essence.

"All manifestations are incomplete or partial expressions of that which can never be fully expressed in any term other than its own; it is the incomprehensible yet all-comprehending: that which could be called God, the Fundamental, Absolute and Eternal Being. This definition may sound formal and formidable to those who are accustomed to cultivating the image of a personal God; yet this same Being is involved in a supremely personal modus operandi with each and every human being. It motivates all life, and directs its undivided and ceaseless attention to every part of creation from the great spheres of light and cauldrons of energy to the tiniest flower unfolding its petals upon the earth.

"This is the Wondrous Being who can count the number of hairs upon a head however lavish the locks, and who notices the fall of a sparrow. It is the all-encompassing and all-governing Being which in splendour is unimaginable, in majesty indescribable, in all-embracing awareness unfathomable. This, the Unknowable is All-Knowing, inaccessible but having access to all. Its veritable essence is the energy-force which functions perpetually to perpetuate life. It emits qualities of perfect order, balance harmony and health, and is constant in its drive towards the repair and renewal of systems and Nature where they have fallen into defect through the uncontrolled vagaries of energies it has released and to which it has allotted self-expression. By its own very nature, this Life-force is free since it is unfettered by limitations and as the sole Life-force is undominated by any opposing force (which is non-existent); it can be understood, therefore, that this

Absolute Freedom characteristically bestows some of this attribute upon many of its creations, and that in these creations, not being complete in knowledge, there are frequent deviations from harmony of function. These deviations give rise to conflict, malformation, confusion, afflictions of mind and body, and subsequent suffering.

"The exploration in an intelligent manner of the psycho-mental aspects of Mankind's being will give the key to many problems of mal-adjustment, ill-health, and conflict between people. The growth of understanding will do much to allay bigotry which is often but the defence of the fearful. The unreasoning and the unreasonable will not be able to lend their minds readily to the acceptance of new ideas: they are their own prisoners; but the free-minded (who are, alas and alack, all too few even in this day and age) will be capable of absorbing fresh facts and elaborating on the possibilities laid before them.

"It will mean the advance of some minds as pioneers who will blaze trails for the rest to follow when they perceive that the new paths are satisfactorily established. There are many who will not commit themselves until they are certain that the world in general will concur. Mankind is beset with a brand of pride which causes it to cower from ridicule, and thins the ranks of those who have the moral stamina to endure the derision of the ignorant, the biased, the self-opinionated, and the apprehensive.

"There are always those who scoff at that which they cannot or will not understand, and the threat of these Philistines may induce hesitation in some people to place before the world new or unusual ideas and experiences. This could hamper the development of communication between the world of spirit and the world of matter, and withhold knowledge that might be gained through diligent application to the subject. True, this attitude of over-scepticism shows signs of modification, but there are still many minds encrusted with crystallised conceptions.

"It is, of course, equally impracticable to be over-credulous; but the credulous by virtue of their very willingness to believe are more likely to be receptive to the truth than their opposite kind. Those who are most likely to block progress in your world are the inveterate sceptics who fondly assume that their immovable intellectualism denotes an ingenious and infallible judgement.

"Finally, a word to the wise, or, more expediently, to the unwise: investigation of psychic faculties as well as mental abilities is a delicate process calling for the utmost prudence, patience, and persistence. Rome was not built in one day nor Everest climbed in one hour; should success not be attained at first, this does not demonstrate that it is impossible to penetrate into these mysteries and unveil their secrets.

"As we look back down the ages, we can detect a repetitive pattern in the past of humanity, a recurrence of sequences which may cause us to remark that we seem to be going round in circles, and, moreover, ominously vicious circles. But in view of man's manifest 20th Century achievements, I would suggest that the circles are ever-widening ones, expanding into time and space in a similar fashion to the ripples travelling outwards from the impact of an object flung into water. I believe our entire outlook and all that it connotes is constantly stretching to encompass new conceptions and unparalleled experiences; I know that human consciousness is spiralling towards greater heights than it has ever before reached in the whole of its history.

"Technical achievements are dangerous unless counter-balanced by added alertness to the problems which they may bring in their train. . . ."

He would have gone on further, but I fear that at this point I was too tired to absorb any more of what he had to say.

One other thing that I have asked Liszt about is suicide in the light of religious teaching.

He says that suicide is something that cannot be generalised about like most things. It is the motive rather than the action by which suicides are judged when they leave this world. He says no-one would condemn anyone who had reached such a pitch of physical or mental suffering that they snapped and put an end to themselves. People like monks who have set fire to themselves to try to stop war would not be judged either; the motive was a good one. But from what Liszt said, I think that people who do cut their lives short so that they are in the spirit world before they are really ready, have to mark time. They are in a suspended state for a period—rather like someone leaving school before they have learnt enough to cope with life.

I wondered how long I had left to do the work Liszt and the others had planned for me and was afraid that perhaps it might be only a few years. I had an enormous sense of urgency about the whole thing. And I felt it was not going to get anywhere before I passed on, if I didn't work very hard. I was afraid that if it were left to other people to do something with the work that was completed, they might feel unable to cope; feel it was not their concern and the music might die with me.

Liszt assured me that I had many years left.

I think perhaps it was because I wanted to know the future for the benefit of other people and how long I had to finish the music that I was allowed to learn that I have enough time to accomplish its main purpose.

It has been suggested to me that I am possibly one of

the most psychic persons living, but I don't think this is true. I am sure there are many, many more who could do my work, but hesitate to attempt it.

All I've done is to try to get to certain levels of consciousness and managed, in a small way, to touch on universal levels which enables one to see truly and have some insight into the eternal realities.

I do not use my mediumship for money. I believe it is a gift from God. I've never set up as a 'professional' medium because for one thing I didn't feel it was my pathway. On the other hand, of course, my mediumship has been used to help others who have been bereaved, or ill, my wish being to give service. But obviously those mediums or healers who devote their whole time to such work have to live, and, I believe, should be recompensed for their time and energy.

The music is something that can be published, and therefore royalties ensue from that. I work hard at it, and hard work does entitle one to some remuneration, and the composers themselves have urged me to accept the royalties.

It is, after all, not possible to live in this world without some money, and the royalties from the music, and indeed, this book, will help me to be freer to continue the work with the composers, and to help others.

And, even more important—I do have my children to bring up.

This is why sometimes the accusations that I am writing the music entirely for money do upset me. And this particular accusation always makes me suspect the accuser of being money-minded himself. As it happens, I am not, and never have been writing the music for money. It is to me a mission, a sacred trust, which the cynics of this world cannot be expected to comprehend.

When the music first began manifesting, had any question of financial gain entered my mind, it is the last thing I would have expected to reap. Classical music, as far as I was aware, was something which obtained little profit if any, although 'pop' music, on the other hand, sometimes brings a fortune to the composer.

I struggled on for years, not knowing whether the music would ever be recognised as compositions from departed composers, and, even if it were, I did not expect to gain financially from any recognition conceded.

In fact, as long as I can earn enough to live a little more comfortably than we have in the past, bring up my children and see them safely on their way into their own lives—this is all I want from life.

CHAPTER SIX

Chopin

Chopin was the second composer whom I met through Liszt and who actually contributed music towards the composers' plan. Next to Liszt, who is by far the most prolific of the contributing composers, I have more music from Chopin than from any of the others. Of course, as, like Liszt, his music is mainly for the piano, it does make it easier to dictate his pieces to me than it is for the other composers like Beethoven who would prefer to compose for a complete orchestra.

When Liszt brought Chopin with him the first time, he very gravely introduced him as: "My friend, M. Frederick Chopin." Chopin then bowed very politely and said: "Enchanté."

He then stood quietly in the background while I sat at the piano with Liszt at my side while we worked together on yet another piece of music. I think Chopin was just there to watch on the first few occasions when he came. He listened very attentively to everything that was going on, and I began to form the impression that he was learning from Liszt how to communicate with me.

One day after they had been together at my home several times, I could hear them talking to each other in English while I jotted down a few bars of music.

Chopin said, with his very strong accent: "She seems very nice, your English girl."

Liszt said carelessly: "Yes, she is quite nice. But she is rather stupid."

I think Liszt had realised that I could hear what they were saying and he had said that deliberately to tease me. So I kept very quiet but I also thought: "Perhaps he is right. I probably do seem rather stupid to them."

It was some days later when they were with me on a different occasion and Liszt was giving me something rather complicated to take down. Funnily enough, the notes were coming quite clearly and easily and I was getting on rather well with the piece.

Suddenly Chopin said: "Your English girl—she is not so stupid." And Liszt laughed—rather as if he were pleased. I guessed then that Chopin had evidently decided that it was all right to work with me. If I could cope with something complicated of Liszt's, therefore, why shouldn't I be intelligent enough to take down his music? And in spite of what Liszt had said about my being stupid, from then on he began to give me music of his own.

These days he often comes alone. At first he always came with Liszt, but as he has proved to be the second best 'communicator'—and quicker even than Liszt—they seem to rather take it in turns to appear. I think they have to watch my progress, and also, for some of the composers, one or the other of them is needed to translate. When I say 'watch my progress' I don't mean that they bother with my daily life of cleaning, and so on, but they have to keep an eye on what is happening in the way of music development, and what is going on with the outside world in relation to their music.

Sometimes Liszt disappears for quite a long time. At first I used to get a little bothered about it, but Chopin was always very soothing. "He has asked me to tell you that he will soon be back," he would say, "I am to take care of things while he is away."

I suppose that there are times when the discarnate beings have to go away from the atmosphere of this world. Not so much the physical but the mental atmosphere. I am sure that they do find our earth pretty harrowing, when you think of all the suffering and strife that goes on. This must affect them, so that they need to have a break and let their consciousness rest a little. They don't get physically tired, of course, because they haven't any physical body to weary. But I think they get a little overtaxed by the contacts with this world. It must require a great deal of effort and I am sure they need time to relax their concentration.

I sometimes find the communication very tiring myself. We have worked out a pattern of work which I try to stick to. Generally, I get the children off to school, do a little housework, and then I'll work on music from about ten until one. Whichever composer is working with me that day then leaves while I eat a bit of lunch, and returns again about half-past one. We then work until about four-thirty when I have to break off to prepare a meal for my children. But the work goes on during the evenings and throughout the weekends, and I give it as much time as I can spare between household chores. I work in my living room because it is the least cold room in the house, and is situated at the rear, away from the road and traffic noise.

I suppose that the composers absorb quite a lot of my attention. Both Chopin and Liszt have taken a great deal of interest in this book, for example. And they've occasionally asked me to correct parts which they don't think are quite clear enough or might give a false impression.

Chopin himself looks very young. About the youngest

of all of them. Around thirty I would say. He has thick, rather wavy hair and a beautiful clear smile which gives him a very youthful appearance. His face is very well-shaped, slightly oval and rather boyish. His eyes are very clear grey-blue. I would have thought they were brown from pictures, but they are actually very noticeably grey-blue.

He, too, likes to wear modern things. Sometimes he arrives in a very splendid cloak, something like an opera cloak, and he seems to pick very deep colours to wear, like deep purples and violet shades. Actually most of the composers like colourful clothing, just in the way that many young people do today.

Another of the things which makes Chopin so appealing is his exquisite manners. He looks and moves like an aristocrat, but it seems very natural somehow—not a pose. I'm sure this is inborn. And really he seems to be patient although he can be excitable—he has been quite cross when someone has been unfair or unkind to me. At first I thought he would think my piano playing was absolutely terrible and go away in disgust. But not at all. Instead he has offered helpful hints on fingering and other matters. It is funny really, because he does not consider himself at all patient, but I find that he is patience itself when working with me.

He is really much too sympathetic to be unkind about anything. If I'm not feeling too well or things are going wrong, he's enormously gentle and thoughtful. I sometimes wonder if this is because he must have suffered himself a great deal. The fact that he had consumption when he was on this earth has, maybe, given him more compassion towards people who are suffering or who are themselves ill.

We talk mostly about music. I do not have the same

type of long discussions with him as I have with Liszt. But Chopin has a very natural, friendly, bantering manner which I am sure is not just put on to make me feel at ease. There is nothing melancholy about him—not like his legend at all. I find him a very light-hearted sort of a person. When he speaks of God, he does so with great reverence, and then I am aware of the deeper, serious side of his nature.

With him I work at the piano and don't hear the music in my head before it comes. The notes gradually evolve. He tells me what the notes and the chords are and then we try it out on the piano. If I'm attempting a chord and my fingers are on the wrong notes, there will be a very gentle pushing and if I let my finger be guided, it goes on to the right note.

Then he says, all pleased: "Ah, zat is right!"

I find this method rather easier than taking down the music by dictation as with that little extra guidance he is getting the notes over to me himself to some extent and it can be much quicker. But much of his new music is too difficult for me to play properly—I stumble through it, just getting some idea of how it should sound.

For example, I was asked to play at the Albert Hall for the 1970 Remembrance Day service, and I asked Chopin if he would give me a new piece of music. It had to be very short as they were only giving me a few minutes.

"Mais oui!" he said immediately, and within the next couple of days he had returned with a brilliant little study. Almost a little too brilliant, I thought. It took me weeks of practice to try to master the piece.

Chopin comes so often to my home that I suppose he can't help getting involved to some extent in our daily lives, I remember one day when he saved us from a flood. My daughter had gone to the bathroom and started to run a bath without my knowledge, and, as youngsters do, had gone away and forgotten all about it. Suddenly Chopin stopped giving me music and said in a very agitated manner: "Le bain va être englouti." He is apt to drop into French when either excited or abstracted, and as my French was solely acquired at school many years ago, I couldn't at first understand what he was saying. However, with so many French-speaking composers visiting me, my knowledge of the language has been forced to improve, and eventually the penny dropped, and I rushed to the bathroom, just in time to stop the water brimming over the top.

He is also very kind about coming to concerts when I am playing. I think he quite enjoys being there, and he is a great moral support as I am still very nervous about playing in public, and not a skilled performer at all.

Some time ago I was very thrilled to get an invitation to visit Leonard Bernstein. He wanted to see some of my music and asked questions about the way I received it. He said to me: "Chopin used to be a very sexy man. Is he still?"

I said: "I don't think so. I've never noticed. But in any case he would not be like that now. Sex is a physical aspect of life which would hardly manifest itself in a non-physical being."

In fact, discarnate beings seem to have no sense of sex or interest in anything of this nature. After death, the earthy side of our being has been left behind. Love expresses itself far more fully and joyfully in other spheres, becoming a thing of greater beauty, enhancing the harmony between friend and loved one.

Because all physical barriers have disappeared, souls who love one another can blend together with an exquisite sense of mingling and unity.

When we are here on earth our real selves are often masked or hidden. We conceal our innermost feelings and thoughts even from those we dearly love. Unreserved communication and complete communion seem too much for most of our human minds to experience. These concealments therefore hamper really attuned exchanges from taking place.

On earth, we see in a glass darkly, but in the other world we are there face to face, and the joy of being able to share consciousness with dear ones, without any barriers, is something that is impossible to describe.

All the many pretences which we learn to live with have gone. We may be shy about our bodies, but to those in the spirit world the human body is no more than a house or a vehicle in which we live and which houses our soul.

In fact, Liszt did mention on one occasion that once we have discarded our physical bodies, sex in the sense that we know it, completely ceases to exist.

You may have guessed that Chopin has a very strong accent, and I had a rather interesting experience regarding that. I belong to the Churches' Fellowship for Physical and Spiritual Studies and I met one of the members, the Reverend Barham, down here in London on a visit from Rugby where he lives.

He asked me what Chopin's voice was like and I tried to describe the timbre and accent to him. It is a rather husky voice but not deep and with a great many inflections in the tone.

Then the Rev. Barham said: "I have a tape recording that I took when I went to see a direct voice medium called Leslie Flint. It seems the person speaking was Chopin. Would you see whether you think it sounds like Chopin or not?"

Well, I knew of Leslie Flint. He is very famous in

psychic circles and very reputable, and naturally I was fascinated to hear if the voice was the same one I had been hearing for the past few years.

It *was* exactly the same. The same pitch, the same strange accent. An accent which is sort of French, but not quite. And when I remarked on that, the Rev. Barham said he had enquired from someone who was a language expert—without revealing whom the voice belonged to—and they had said it was English spoken with a Slav-French accent. Which would make sense because Chopin was half Polish.

Also, listening to the tape, the same sort of bantering manner that he adopts was coming through and I was convinced it really was Chopin.

One of the people who was at the meeting when the tape was made said: "You're Polish, aren't you? Say something in Polish."

And Chopin said in that droll way of his: "Ah, now you are testing me!" And apparently did not oblige with any Polish. But he has spoken this language to me at times. It is difficult to pick up the sound and repeat it, but I have sometimes managed a few words, although I expect I pronounce them badly.

Once when he was giving me some music, I think someone else must have been trying to interrupt, and he said, quite crossly, some words which I jotted down phonetically. When I checked them with a Polish acquaintance I found they meant, quite simply: "You go away!"

There are two sequels to the Leslie Flint story. Firstly, one afternoon I was watching TV with a quick cup of tea when I suddenly had a feeling that I ought to switch to the other channel—the Eamonn Andrews programme. My son, Thomas, wasn't very pleased because he preferred the other programme, but my hunch was quite strong so I switched over to the other TV channel.

I found they were just about to begin a programme about Leslie Flint. There, on the screen, was a picture of Chopin and a tape-recording of his voice was being played.

Of course, after the tape was finished there were a lot of questions asked, and I thought Leslie Flint spoke out very bravely and calmly and said what a pity it is that people—and very often the ones you would think would be interested—seem to want to do everything possible to disprove any kind of contact with the other world, instead of trying to think about the evidence and give it a chance.

They played tapings of two or three other people as well—Oscar Wilde, and Ellen Terry, as I remember. And then the usual question came: "Why is it always famous people?"

Leslie Flint gave the same answer that I do. It is *not* always famous people, but if the beings who have come through are someone's friend or relative and unknown to the world, they don't mean a thing to the public at large. People who are famous and known to the public are more interesting because one can check up more easily on them than is possible with totally unknown voices. And besides, as I think I have already mentioned, it is the most extrovert people who seem to be able to break through to our world with the least difficulty. And very often fame and being an extrovert are inclined to go hand in hand.

The second sequel to the Leslie Flint story is that I became so intrigued with hearing Chopin's voice through another medium of communication that I had some "sittings" with Mr. Flint myself. They were incredibly successful; Chopin, Beethoven, Liszt, and Sir Henry Wood (who does occasionally visit me) all coming through and reiterating their reasons for the work. Clara Schumann, surprisingly, also came through, and equally surprisingly, Liszt seemed to have the most difficulty making contact with the direct voice method. He complained that it was very difficult, and that he had become so used to speaking with me direct he found it much harder this way.

Chopin, on the other hand, has obviously completely mastered the direct voice method. He chatted away, and became very cross with me in his bantering fashion because I called him Monsieur Chopin.

"What is all this 'Monsieur Chopin'?" he said, his voice rising. "If you do not call me Frederick, I will not call you Rosemary!" (He pronounces my name as "Rose-marie".)

But all of them stressed again the importance of the work I am doing for them and said how glad they were that the results were beginning to be seen by the outside world. And you can imagine how comforting it was to me to hear that confirmed—and entirely through the work of another medium.

CHAPTER SEVEN

The Composers

All of the composers who have been to see me have, in the first instance, arrived accompanied by Liszt. He introduces them to me because, as I have already explained, he is the organiser of this group of musicians who have been using me to work with them. Often, after the first introduction, they come on their own to see me. After the first few meetings with a newly-arrived composer, Liszt becomes less involved, though I have noticed that even when they begin to work with me quite independently he is generally there somewhere in the background, watching to see how things go, and ready to translate, should it be necessary.

Brahms does seem to come quietly and totally on his own occasionally, though it is possible that Liszt knows he is with me. It seems to me that all of them have to fall in with some kind of plan and take their turn to communicate. It is as if they have to go to Liszt and ask for permission to work with me. I think perhaps he acts as a sort of guardian to make certain I'm not too inundated with demands from the various composers. Which is just as well or otherwise I'd never get a moment's peace. As it is, when I am at my own home they keep me very busy.

Schubert and Beethoven came to see me together on the first occasion. Liszt, of course, accompanied them to make the introductions. And I seem to remember that the first time I saw Schubert he was wearing spectacles. I'm sure that was only to help me to identify him because obviously they do not need glasses on their side, and he never wears them when he comes to see me now.

I noticed that Schubert was really quite handsome, particularly as he does not have that 'puffy', rather jowly look which seems to characterise him in all his photographs. When I did the London Weekend Aquarius programme, they produced a photograph of Schubert without spectacles for me, and though he still looked rather chubby it was possible to see that he was also quite handsome in life.

One of the things I like the most about him is his expression. His eyes are very soft and seem to beam friendliness. He is extremely modest and self-effacing; quiet and yet merry in a way, though his sense of humour is rather old-fashioned. He doesn't crack jokes, but he is bubbling over with good humour and obviously has a great sense of fun. I think he would have had that here on earth as well. I'm sure this twinkly personality is not something that has just come to him because he is released from this world.

I find Schubert lovable. I think everyone would like him. His modesty is very appealing and he never changes. He is not in the least moody. Liszt is quite different. When Liszt is in a voluble mood the words won't come out fast enough, but at other times he can be quite solemn and silent. Schubert, on the other hand, is always the same. Modest, merry and very kind.

It was in 1966 when he and Beethoven came first to see me. It is easy for me to remember when they all first appeared as I always date their music as I set it down.

So far, Schubert has given me a piano sonata, Sonata in C Major, which covers about forty pages. I think it is a beautifully flowing piece—not too easy, nor yet too difficult to play. He has also given me about eight songs, mostly with words. For the greater part, he has tried to give me the words in 'German, but I find it is very difficult to take down as I've never had any German lessons at all.

One of these songs was used on a B.B.C. One TV programme. Dr. Troupe, who is a very fine musician and a teacher at the Guildhall School of Music, played the piece and he asked one of the Guildhall Students to sing it.

I have several parts of string quartets from Schubert, none finished as yet, as obviously any piece of music for more than one instrument takes much longer to dictate to me. There is also a section of a piece of music for orchestra and we are also working on an opera which I am afraid will be an awful slog to take down for him. I already have a few passages of it, and very striking the music is. He has used some very strange harmonies and I shall have to show what I have to someone who is more knowledgeable to get it explained to me. Schubert hasn't chosen a known story for the plot of his opera. It is an original idea about life after death and how life goes on and can triumph over death. He is also very fond of weaving that particular theme into his songs. One that is not yet completed, but that I particularly like, goes:

> "Softly falls the winter snow;
> Bleak blows the blizzard that drives it to and fro.
> Can there be hope in a world that's so cruel?
> Can springtime follow? Can flowers blossom?
> Can there be life after death's bitter sorrow?
> Wilt thou rewaken in heaven tomorrow?"

He seems to be trying to make people realise that perhaps there is something else to look forward to. I think he wants to give us hope.

Incidentally, when we are working on his songs he sometimes tries to sing them to me. I'm afraid he hasn't a very good voice. I would have thought that when they arrived over there everyone would have immediately been given a good singing voice—but his disproves that theory. He has a fairly soft voice—a tenor pitch, I'd say—not deep. And he speaks with an accent. It is rather thick and sometimes so bad that I can't understand what he is saying and I have to get him to repeat it.

Schubert is one of the composers who does appear in other places than my home. I remember on one occasion when I went to Attingham Park in the summer of 1967 for one of Mary Firth's courses that she gives there at the College for Adult Education. She and I had become quite friendly by then after our original meeting through the Wontners and Sir George, and as on this occasion she was running a course on Schubert, I went thinking it might help with my understanding of his music.

One of the pieces she was covering was the C Major Symphony, which I didn't know at all. All the students at the course are asked to follow a score, and Mary explains exactly how to do this.

She does this mainly for the benefit of the newer students who are just beginning to learn music appreciation and theory. A few of the people who go there are like I was, more or less starting from scratch, though the bulk of the students who attend her courses are either music teachers, people who are qualified in music to some degree or full time students of music. Those with my sort of limited technical knowledge are actually rather rare at Attingham.

However, once the explanation of how to follow a score is completed, the main purpose of the lesson begins. A small section of whichever piece is being studied is played on the record-player, and then Mary Firth has the machine stopped, explains what the music is doing and points out the various instruments which are being used, explaining the rôles of strings, etc. Then she asks questions. All of this is to understand the music and point out all the wonderful nuances that one might miss by just listening casually.

She was going through Schubert's symphony in this way when suddenly I saw that he was standing beside me. He said, in his heavily accented English: "Will you make a note of that passage—" pointing out to me a few bars of music played by one of the wind instruments on the score that I was holding.

"What for?" I asked, putting a little pencil mark by the notes he had indicated.

"You will see," he said.

As the lesson progressed, Mary Firth eventually stopped the record-player and asked if anybody could pick out a certain section in the piece we had just heard which was rather unusual.

There was a long silence. No-one from the fifty or so people who were there—most of them highly qualified musicians—spoke.

She looked a bit quizzical and then said: "I'll buy to-night's glass of sherry for whoever answers the question correctly."

There was a long silence and she said: "Doesn't anybody know?"

Well, at this point, Schubert gave me a nudge and said: "Go on. It's that passage I asked you to note. Tell her."

So I gathered up my courage and said rather diffidently: "Could it be these bars?" And pointed them out to her.

Mary was very surprised, because I was quite correct,

and she knows perfectly well that I am a bit dim about things like that, especially in an orchestral score as I have had no orchestral training. Fortunately, she did not ask me what was unusual about the passage, but I gathered afterwards it was something to do with the fact that one theme (or subject as they call it) was tucked away rather secretly in one of the wind instruments' pieces and hard to spot. Dr. Firth himself was sitting next to me, and even he had not spoken up. Possibly he knew the answer, although he had remained silent.

Later on that evening, when we all gathered for dinner and the sherry was being served (which we had to pay for separately), Mary said to me: "Come on. You must have your glass of sherry."

"Schubert ought to have it really," I told her.

She looked a bit puzzled.

"Why?" she asked.

"Because he told me to mark that passage a long time before you asked the question," I told her. "I wanted to know why, but all he'd say was 'You will see'. And then when you asked the question he was nudging me and saying: 'Go on. Tell her'."

However, as the glass of sherry could not be made available to Schubert at this point of his existence, I drank it on his behalf, toasting him with my thanks.

I'm no expert on Schubert—nor any of the others come to that. Mary Firth is, and I know she likes Schubert's music very much. He knows that she has a soft spot for him and he is pleased by her regard for his work. I suspect, in fact, that is why he came to that particular course with me.

I have actually heard the end of the Unfinished Symphony, and it is very, very beautiful. Schubert let me hear it by telepathy. Several of the composers can do this, and they can also 'compress' time in such a way that I can actually hear an entire concerto or symphony in minutes. Eventually I hope to be able to write down the last movement of the Unfinished for Schubert—but I am afraid it will be a long and difficult task.

Schubert is not a very talkative person. I think he is really a bit too shy to say very much. But even so, the more I know of Schubert, the more I love him. I feel a deep affection for him. He's somehow very easy to get on with and I feel at home with him. Not in any romantic sense, of course. It's the feeling that one would have for an older brother or a very dear uncle. Love—but not romantic love, in case anyone should get far-fetched ideas!

I wish I could say the same for Bach. But I don't really like working with him very much. He is very stern and doesn't seem to have any sense of humour at all. I've never seen him smile once, and he's inclined to be rather straightlaced. Or perhaps it's only with me.

When he comes to the house it's just for work, work, work. I've rarely seen him away from my own home and he never talks about anything but music when he is there.

Like the others, Liszt brought him to the house the first time, and he explained to him that he would probably find it difficult to communicate. He also more or less cautioned him to go gently, which was thoughtful of him because I would think that Bach is a very strong character and could be rather domineering.

I remember on the first occasion, when Liszt decided it was all right to leave Bach to work alone with me, Liszt's parting remark was: "Do not cross her will." Bach said nothing but settled down to work.

At the time, I thought this was rather an odd thing to say, and that perhaps Liszt was trying to say politely: "Don't be too forceful."

But Bach is forceful. I have a tremendous admiration and respect for him, but I haven't been able to get close to him. He speaks some English which I would think he's taught himself on the other side as I don't expect he spoke English here. I'd like to ask him, but I wouldn't dare! I couldn't look upon him as a friend and go to him for advice or help. I just have to take the music that he gives me and that's that. It is strictly a teacher-pupil relationship. I feel all the time that I'm being given a very formal music lesson.

Even in spirit he looks very similar to all the pictures one sees of him, except that he seems to be rather less weighty now. He appears to be aged about forty. Some pictures, for example, make him look very heavy jowled, and now this is not so. But on the whole, he's easily recognisable from pictures.

He sometimes dresses in clothes of his own time, but surprisingly, he'll sometimes appear in something more modern. He is, of course, one of the earliest of my composers. He's always very neat and tidy in his appearance, but I get the feeling that he is not in the least interested in how he looks. Everything he wears is rather nondescript looking. He never seems to go in for bright colours—he wears mostly browns and greys—whereas most of the other composers like to wear coloured waistcoats and bright cravats. But Bach is always rather sombre in his dress.

I've had a fair amount of music from him, but not nearly as much as from Liszt, Chopin or Schubert. And all the pieces I have had from Bach are fairly short. He hasn't given me anything very long yet, and I suspect this is because he doesn't want to dwell on the type of music he wrote when he was here.

Now he has given me enough pieces to establish his

signature, I think he wants to progress on to something quite different. I have one or two pieces from him which I think that people might not recognise as Bach at all.

I myself still feel intuitionally an echo of his work in them, but this latest music he is producing has gone on to harmonies and ideas which I doubt if he would have used in his lifetime. The last music I took from him was a short piano piece which was really modern in style.

The one good thing about working with Bach is that he is quick and he is exact. He is able to get his ideas over to me very clearly. He must have a very methodical mind. He dislikes my working at the piano, and he prefers just to tell me the notes. I really prefer to use the piano and sometimes I try to slip over to it to play over what he is giving me. I think he disapproves and regards this as time wasting. Or perhaps he does not like my playing much!

Perhaps when I've worked with him more I may feel more at ease. But I do find him rather awe-inspiring. But then, he does have an awe-inspiring talent, and I believe his new type of music—if he can transmit it—could arouse a fair amount of interest in the music world. What is so fascinating is that even though he died in 1750, his musical ideas are more modern.

Now, Rachmaninov is different again. When he first came to see me I thought I could never take to him. He's not exactly stern—sort of poker-faced rather than severe, and when he does smile it comes rather slowly and then lingers. Quite different from Liszt's smile. That flashes. Suddenly Liszt's whole face lights up, whereas with Rachmaninov it's almost as if he thinks and takes his time beside deciding that a smile is in order. And when he smiles, I noticed that he is inclined to move his head as well.

He does speak English, of course, but occasionally when he forgets or is excited, I've managed to catch an occasional word of Russian from him. I write it down and try to work out what it means afterwards, but it isn't easy as, of course, I have to write whatever he says phonetically.

After a cool beginning I now like him very much, and we do sometimes talk about subjects other than music. I find him friendly now, though at first he was rather stiff and formal. I asked him once about Russia and what he thought about his country today.

I think he must be patriotic even now, because he answered very carefully.

"Russia is a very great country," he said, "and she will become even greater if she practises non-aggression."

And he didn't seem to want to say any more than that.

As well as giving me music, Rachmaninov seems to spend a lot of time here with me in helping with my piano technique. He was very insistent that I begin to practise chromatic sixths, which are very difficult to do. He gave me his own method of fingering to practise while trying these. Shortly after, in 1967, which was about the time when Rachmaninov first appeared, I started to have piano lessons again in order to be able to play the composers' music with more skill. I told my teacher—without mentioning Rachmaninov of course, that I wanted to practise chromatic sixths.

"Why not?" he said. "If you really want to practise them, this is what you do."

And he gave me some fingering which was entirely different from that Rachmaninov had suggested. I think that Rachmaninov in life may have used rather individual methods.

He's quite a hard taskmaster. He has had me practising other techniques, like chromatic crossing thirds. These are absolutely appalling to play. You start two octaves apart and in thirds, moving with both hands, come closer and closer until you cross in the middle with the right hand on top and continue the thirds. Then you must cross with the left hand on top. As you can imagine I'm not keen on playing them. He has his own particular fingerings which he says are better for technique and facilitates playing.

"I would always use fingering that makes for easier playing than that which is regarded as correct," he told me once. He doesn't bother much about expression when he's giving me a lesson. That and interpretation are left to Liszt to infuse into my piano playing. It is speed and brilliance that Rachmaninov concentrates on, and if we both had the time to give to it, I think he could make a great deal of improvement in my playing. But it isn't possible to take the time when I'm trying to take down composition from all the other composers and write out neatly all the pieces that I've already scribbled down.

Rachmaninov has also tried to 'get some style' into my playing and if I completely dropped the composition side of the work and just studied under him, I'm sure he could make me sound quite good.

He stands very patiently beside me while I play. I've never seen him sit. Liszt, Chopin and Schubert all do sit down sometimes, and Beethoven has once or twice when he was talking to me. I must say that it is rather extraordinary when they sit. But I suppose they only do it to create a relaxed atmosphere.

Rachmaninov's face is rather long and thin, and he looks much more severe than he really is. But he is very compassionate, I think because he has suffered himself. He told me that there was a period in his life when he felt utterly rejected as a person and as a musician. He just laid down and hoped to die, and then gradually his confidence began to be restored and he felt that maybe he would write great music, in spite of what the wretched critics had had to say about his work.

I've mentioned earlier in this book that the spirits do seem to have some foreknowledge. There was a morning when I was terribly busy. I had all my shopping to do and I'd literally got my coat on to go out when Rachmaninov appeared, asking to finish a piece of music we had already been working on.

"Oh, I can't stop now," I said. "I simply haven't time."

He was very insistent, and persuaded me to sit down, and then said: "It's important you take this composition. You will need it this evening, and I wish to give it a conclusion."

He wouldn't tell me *why* I'd need his music and I wasn't sure whether or not to believe him. When the composers have a new piece to communicate they are inclined to be rather demanding and not to be put off under any circumstances no matter how inconvenient. Anyway, rather reluctantly I agreed to take the music down and fortunately we got it done quite quickly. When he had stopped dictating, he told me the piece was really longer, but he had finished that section so it could be played as a complete part. Then he said good-bye, with the parting remark—accompanied by one of his rare smiles: "Don't forget to take that with you tonight. It is important."

As far as I knew then, I was not going anywhere that evening. I had invited some friends to supper, and was left in the dark about the mysterious event he hinted at before he left.

However, he was quite correct. Later in the day, my agent, Barry Krost, sent me a telegram asking me to telephone him. I popped out to the phone-box around the corner, got through to Barry's office, and was told that

Leonard Bernstein, the American composer, was in London, staying at the Savoy and would like me to have supper with him and his wife that evening at 11 o'clock.

"And," Barry added, "take some scores with you."

Well, I was a little flustered by the whole idea. I felt that eleven o'clock was very late to be going out, and I didn't own the right clothes for visits to the Savoy or to meet people like the Bernsteins. I hummed and hawed on the telephone until Barry, deciding I was quite mad to hesitate to take an opportunity to meet one of the most famous composers in the world, said: "Don't be silly. Of course you must go. We'll send a car to pick you up about 10.30 p.m."

When I was collecting a few scores to take that evening after accepting the invitation (which fortunately I was able to do as the supper date had been postponed anyway), Rachmaninov reappeared briefly to remind me to take that particular score we had been working on in the morning. He said he thought Mr. Bernstein would be especially interested in it. So I did what he said.

Eleven o'clock that night found me arriving at the Savoy, clutching some of the composers' music, including Rachmaninov's piece.

I was ushered into Mr. Bernstein's suite to find him taking a meal with his wife, and with Erik Smith, who is the son of Hans Schmidt-Isserstedt, the conductor, his wife, and my agent. Mr. Bernstein had been working very hard all the evening conducting, but he was full of life and welcomed me in a most friendly way. I was rather overawed, but he soon made me feel more at ease with his warmth and personality.

"Now, what will you have to drink?" he asked. "Of course, you can have anything, but here in my suite we have only whisky and vodka."

I had drunk neither previously, and hesitated, not sure what to say.

"Here, try this," he said suddenly, and thrust his own glass into my hand. I sipped the contents, wondering how many people had ever had the honour of drinking from the same glass as this great conductor. It was whisky, so he informed me, and I found it rather strong in taste; Erik Smith offered to fix me a milder version.

"Would you care for some chicken—it's very good," Mr. Bernstein went on, "or the shrimps here—they are simply delicious? Oh, I wish I hadn't thought of them. Now I want some!"

There were waiters discreetly attending to all his needs, and no sooner had he mentioned that he wanted shrimps than a trolley was wheeled in with an ample supply beautifully served. It seemed to me that he was very popular with the waiters, and I had the impression it was not just because he was famous and affluent, but because they really liked him for himself.

Presently he asked me what music had I brought, and I produced a number of scores from the brief case I had with me. He persuaded me to play, which I did with some trepidation, aware of my limitations of technique. Then he asked to have some of the scores to play himself. It became apparent that he is a marvellous pianist as well as a great conductor. He liked very much the 'Fantaisie-Impromptu' in three movements which I had received from Chopin; in fact, he liked a great many of the pieces, Liszt's, Schubert's, Beethoven's, and the Rachmaninov which, as the composer had predicted, interested him very much. It was a vivacious piece, very chromatic in nature —a real concert study—and Mr. Bernstein took to it greatly, and played it with great brilliance and remarkable speed, rolling out some of the passages like thunder. It sounded splendid, and I wished that I could make it sound as wonderful. There was only one piece he didn't seem to like: "That's the only bar I don't buy," were his exact words. But Rachmaninov has since embellished that, so perhaps he would 'buy' it now.

In the Chopin Fantaisie-Impromptu, there is a lovely theme at one point which caught the ear of both Mr. Bernstein and his wife. They had it played over several times as if they wanted to memorise it. I hope this item of Chopin's will be put on record eventually because it meant a great deal of hard work and patience on his part and mine, and has been hailed as typically Chopin and very unified in structure.

Chopin said that in his lifetime it had been commented that some of his works were flung together in a disjointed fashion; this work, he said, would perhaps demonstrate that he was capable of a composition of unity. I have noticed some of the composers can sometimes still be sensitive to criticism and have more than once hoped they were not disappointed when there have been comments of a derogatory or belittling nature.

One has to take all criticism in one's stride, remembering that it is not always well-judged and may sometimes even be tinged with jealousy. But it has been a great joy to Chopin and the others to find that most of the compositions they have given me are really appreciated for their beauty, whether simple—as a few of them are—or very complicated—as many are. There are pieces which need a pianist of virtuoso standing to perform them really well.

I felt quite like Cinderella that night when I met Mr. Bernstein at the Savoy—especially recalling my days of menial labour in the school kitchens! He is such a charming and kindly man, and must be much loved as well as much admired; and his wife was equally charming and kind. Before I left, he gave me some tickets to attend the recording of the Verdi Requiem at St. Paul's Cathedral two nights later. This was a work I had never heard—in common with many other works of the great composers —and I was spellbound by the beautiful, moving music, and Mr. Bernstein's phenomenal conducting which is a sheer delight to watch.

I suppose you could call Rachmaninov a slightly austere person in some ways. Quite the reverse is another of the composers—Debussy. When TV presented his life some time ago, I watched the film with great interest, but somehow the programme did not entirely add up to the man who visits me fairly regularly to give me his new music.

I find Debussy a very amusing sort of person. He likes to dress in what my daughter called kinky clothes, and he does appear to be flamboyant. Once he came in a sheepskin jacket with a straw hat perched on his head. He obviously enjoys wearing this sort of clothing, and it does rather suit him.

He is usually pictured with a beard, but he is clean-shaven now, with a rather pallid skin, and quite a lot of very dark hair growing away from an imposing forehead. His eyes are rather dark, and his voice is deep. Sometimes, with the effort of trying to communicate, it can sound a little harsh. He is quite serious in temperament. He hardly ever laughs and rarely smiles. He is certainly not a humorous person, though he can be quite witty on occasions.

Sometimes I think he is the most original of all the composers who work through me. This originality comes out in both his thinking and his habits, so much so that I do find him rather uncomfortable to be with for any length of time. I suppose he embarrasses me just a little. Liszt is always saying that I'm inclined to be prim and proper, and I find I am more relaxed with people who are inclined to be conventional.

However, Debussy is a very deep thinker, which could explain his extraordinary life—if it was truly like that TV programme. People who think deeply often are unorthodox, I've found. When people think for themselves instead of accepting the ideas that are already laid down, it does lead them to appear unconventional. I suppose that, like Liszt, Debussy, too, was a victim of manners of his period. Thousands of people now live the sort of life he lived then —wearing bizarre clothes and sometimes sleeping with women who are not their wives. Today, no-one takes much notice. Then it was different.

Though I don't personally believe Debussy was as wild as he is often painted, and that nowadays he would not seem so eccentric.

Liszt once told me that Debussy holds the view that God is an infinity. As I have already mentioned, they still have their own religious views over there, and they do not all have the answers, though some think they are close to the truth. Liszt says there are people who have reached the highest levels where they know the final truth, but they cannot always communicate this to those who are not so advanced mainly because they would not be able to grasp the entirety.

He says that in a sense Debussy is right when he says God is an infinity, but it is a word that could mislead us here because it is perhaps too vague.

Debussy is not a regular visitor of mine. He's somewhat mercurial. Sometimes he'll be in and out for days, and then I won't see him for a long time.

I've had a fair number of piano pieces from him, and he has begun work on a septet which hasn't got very far yet. It is for strings and wind instruments and the middle of the piece seems rather original and arresting. I think it's going to be intriguing, but my son Thomas doesn't like it. I play the themes on the piano and every time I play them Thomas shrinks because he feels the music is rather discordant.

I've also had some songs from Debussy and the words of these are to come from someone called Lamartine, who was a writer in life, and who is on the other side now, with Debussy and the others.

There was an occasion when I went up to Attingham Park for one of Mary Firth's lectures. One free period, I slid into the lecture room where there is a fine Steinway piano and played a little of a new Debussy piece that he had given me a few days before.

One of the students at dinner that night said: "I heard you playing some Debussy this afternoon."

I laughed and said: "It wasn't anything that Debussy wrote when he was here."

"Oh, come," the young man said. "I'm a Debussy student. I'd know his work anywhere. I recognised it immediately."

That was a young man called Derek Watson who is now at Edinburgh University studying music. I thought that little incident very encouraging, because, to me, though the work that Debussy is giving me may be changing from the style in which he wrote while on earth, it is still recognisable as his music in some instances.

But perhaps the most fascinating thing regarding Debussy is that he has started to paint now he is on the other side. And he has shown me his work. He'll just say: "I have a picture," and present it. He never asks whether or not I want to see what he has done, though, of course, he probably realises how interested I am.

The pictures are very beautiful and it is a great pity

that the world can't see them. He is so proud of them himself, that I wish some way could be found for them to be shown.

The first one I saw was entirely in different shades of blue. At first, all I could see was all this mass of blue, and I thought to myself—"Well, the colours are beautiful, but what *is* it?"

Then, as I looked harder, I began to realise there was a woman's face in the middle of the picture. Even her skin was pale blue, and her hair deeper blue, but it was all so misty that it was not possible to see the face at first.

He has also painted a pair of pictures 'Sunrise' and 'Sunset'. They, of course, are in all the sun colours—predominately red and reddish orange. He never seems to use any kind of contrasts in his pictures and the latest one I've seen is predominately purple, but shades of purple that seem to melt into a purplish brown. I've only caught a glimpse of this painting, and I want very much to see it again. It is the darkest of all his pictures so far, and I think it contains peacock feathers merged unobtrusively into the painting.

He has given me a piece of music which he called 'The Peacock' and the picture reminded me of this particular piece of music. I'm sure the two go together as there are eyes painted into the feathers, as on a peacock's tail. But in his painting he has made them look like real eyes. This is rather disconcerting as some of the eyes are looking straight out, and directly at the viewer, while others look sideways. It is a curious painting, but very original.

More relaxing company than Debussy is Brahms who first came to see me with Liszt, of course, in 1968. I like Brahms. I'm very much at ease with him. He has extraordinary patience and usually manages to communicate without any difficulty, sustaining the 'link' for long periods at a time. Others of the composers who come, particularly Debussy, seem unable to work with me for very long periods.

I find Brahms a very serene person, and yet there is something very strong about him. He is rather a mixture in some ways. He has a certain modest quality, and yet there is an air of quiet confidence about him. For example, if Schubert gives me a piece, he will say afterwards, quite anxiously: "Do you like it?" It is as if he is a little uncertain; needing reassurance—and definitely not bouncing with confidence.

On the other hand, when Brahms gives me a piece of music—that is that. He is not really concerned whether I like it or not.

I have had quite a lot of music from Brahms, mainly for the piano, and there was one piece of his on the first LP that Philips made. I've also been given some string quartets by him, and it was a part of one of these that was played at the end of a B.B.C. documentary. He has also begun to introduce wind instruments into his music occasionally, but so far this is only in the development stage.

Because of the string quartets, I have to take much of his music down by hand. I remember the first time he arrived with the intention of giving me music I was sitting at the piano. I played what he gave me as well as I could but it became difficult as he uses tenths rather a lot. My hands, unfortunately, are too small to stretch this far, though I can manage better than I used to. I think that Brahms must have had an extraordinary span between his fingers when he was here. I find he will want me to play two notes about four notes apart with two fingers—and my hands won't stretch to it. I'm trying to improve, but I get so little time to practise technique.

Brahms is one of the ones who speak fairly good English.

He said that he had a friend who taught him the language —I don't know who it was. He said rather cryptically it was someone he met in our world who is now in his world.

In our conversations, he keeps entirely to music. He is not one of the people with whom I can chat about other matters. He has made little remarks occasionally, but basically his interests in coming to see me is to communicate his music.

One day, he arrived with Clara Schumann, and I thought, obviously adoring her. He had his arm around her in a most tender and protective way. She, of course, was Robert Schumann's wife, and it seems to me that though she still has great devotion for her husband, she shares an enormous affinity with Brahms.

Obviously there is no marriage as we know it on the other side. If one has many friends of the same sex in this world, it is considered perfectly all right, whereas there, if one has several friends of the opposite sex it becomes equally acceptable as a different sort of relationship. Therefore, I was not really surprised when Clara Schumann arrived in my work room with Brahms.

She explained that she wanted to give me some music that had been written by her husband—apparently at first he didn't want to come himself. Later on he did appear, just once or twice, but I find he is very elusive and poor at communicating. Clara, on the other hand, comes over very clearly.

But then she is a firm little person; rather strong-willed. Schumann, when he was on earth, became mentally unbalanced we are told, and it is possible that that may have made her more emphatic in temperament, as perhaps one does in the face of difficulties.

Her husband was—and is—very different. I don't think he likes to come himself with the music. I suspect that he is just a little embarrassed at trying to communicate, just as I'm a little embarrassed at playing for an audience. Also, I don't think his powers of concentration as regards communication are very good really. His mind is inclined to wander off, and he becomes absorbed in something quite different from the music he has to give.

I imagine the difficulty is that he is not sufficiently extroverted. As I have said before, it does seem that it is those who are extroverts in life who are best able to communicate with us who are here on earth.

It is, I have been told, a known fact that Schumann was an introverted person, and not sufficiently out-going to converse freely with others. Now Clara is much more of an extrovert, though I haven't had a great deal of music from either her or her husband. He comes, as a rule, with Liszt. I've never seen Schumann and Clara together yet. But in life, Brahms became a friend of both of them, and when Schumann went into hospital he tried to look after Clara. They never married after Schumann's early death. I think Brahms so much respected Schumann's memory that he felt it might be too intrusive to marry his widow.

However, I am afraid I don't feel close to her. She seems to be rather a dominating person. But then perhaps she became like that as a result of all the trouble she had in life. It must have been terrible for her when her husband went out of his mind as they were very much in love with each other. Her life cannot have been easy for she lived for many years after his death. Very often, people are called hard when it is only some tragedy or loss that had made them assume an attitude of self-defence against life's troubles.

But even so, there isn't much sympathy between us. She doesn't seem very feminine to me, though I must admit she has a very definite style of her own.

She seems to like fairly short dresses for herself. She usually wears something about mid-calf length and she doesn't keep to the nineteenth century clothes which she would have worn on earth. At present this mid-calf length may indeed prove fashionable as there are moves in the fashion world to bring skirts nearer to the ground.

I rather think she likes to design her own clothes, and in the way that Debussy has taken up painting, she has taken up dress designing. She often dresses slightly in the fashion of the ancient Greeks with cross-over bodices, but with little puff-sleeves added. I've noticed she likes light colours—her favourite seems to be a sort of creamy shade. I've never seen her wearing anything dark in tone.

She seems to be fond of shiny fabrics. Most of her clothes are in rather satiny looking materials. One other thing that I've noticed about her is that when she smiles the top teeth are very slightly overshot, but pretty.

But it is no good hiding one's feelings. I don't really feel at ease with her.

One of the wonderful things about the work I am doing is this opportunity to get to know something of the people I work with and in some cases come to love them.

I have a very great love for Liszt, Chopin, Schubert, Beethoven and also—Rachmaninov. Yet at first I never felt I could feel any warmth for Rachmaninov at all. He seemed so reserved and inaccessible. But by now I feel a wonderful friendship towards him.

In the summer of 1970, he told me that communication would become very much easier between us—and now it is. I have no idea what happened to make the change as originally I found communication with him difficult. But now he comes over very clearly when he is present—but he disappears for weeks on end between concentrated periods of work.

For a long time Beethoven was an enigma to me. At first, he would communicate just by telepathy. He would impress the music on my mind without speaking a word. I could see him, but nothing was ever said by either of us. Most of the time I would find I could slowly catch hold of his ideas, although he would never name a note, yet I would just somehow know what he wanted to convey.

I think that perhaps the original communication might have been difficult and slow in coming because I was in terrific awe of him. He is an awe-inspiring person to look at, and there is no doubt that he was one of the greatest souls to live in this world.

He appears to be between thirty-five and forty when he comes to see me now. He has a very fine shaped head with a rather Greek look about it. His skin is good now, and he has very black hair which he wears swept back off his forehead. It is not so bushy now as it is in pictures of him, but it is still worn fairly long. His features are even, and his eyes very dark. And they are direct eyes which look straight at you.

Of course, he is no longer deaf. Those human ills and frailties disappear once we reach the other side. It was his deafness and illness which we can well imagine may have made him appear stormy-natured in life. One needs to look beyond the earthly personality which was a re-action to the circumstances of his life, as it may often be with many. To say he was not good-tempered negates the true greatness of the man, but this irritability was no more than a personality trait, and nothing to do with the real soul at all.

At first, in those silent meetings, I had a strong sense of this greatness; this real nobility of soul. The room was full of an atmosphere of sanctity. And I think it was feel-ing this atmosphere so strongly that at first overwhelmed me so that I was insufficiently at ease with him for much conversation to take place. But gradually I began to realise that Beethoven has, in fact, a great simplicity which is truly sublime. And having realised that I became a little more confident in my attitude towards him. This perhaps encouraged him to begin to talk to me, and he began to speak in English, quite slowly, using short, easy words, and sentences in a very simple way, almost as if he were talking to a child—which I probably seem to be to him.

Gradually a bond of sympathy began to spring up between us. I felt that though he was far above me, he did understand me. And I felt tremendously honoured that he would just stand there talking to me. Sometimes he talks about music, and sometimes he will talk about himself or life—or God. He says now he longs to pour forth great torrents of music which would really stir us into greater understanding; he wants to pour out his music for us in fountains of compassion. And he makes me feel that he aches to reach out to humanity and enfold us in wonderful love. He has an intense devotion to and belief in God with no narrowness in his thinking at all, and one day he was talking to me so gently and quietly that I felt very moved and very humble, and I said to him: "Beethoven—I love you."

He just looked at me with the suspicion of a smile and said quite seriously: "Of course."

As far as his music is concerned, he has been giving me scoring for different parts of a symphony, but it is very complicated to follow and I find it a slow and laborious business. It would, of course, be very difficult to take this type of music dictation down from someone who was actually *here* in the flesh. Our two different dimensions make it much harder.

Mary Firth once told me that even her quite advanced

students would find it difficult if she dictated something to them note by note. She said, it is just not easy to write music down in this way.

"No wonder you find it difficult when you are trying to take the notes down from someone on another level," she said to me once.

Yet, sometimes, the communication is very quick and simple. I think perhaps there may be a certain amount of automatic writing involved. For example, when Peter Dorling was making the B.B.C. film and asked me if I could work with one of the composers, I found that Beethoven was there. Now, at the time, I was working away from the piano, just sitting at the table with music manuscript and a pencil in my hand. The music suddenly started to come very rapidly and I think Beethoven gave me about six or eight bars of left hand straight off. The notes were almost writing themselves, so I think possibly there was some kind of 'control' going on. The right hand came immediately afterwards. But that is a thing that does happen to me. And I would imagine it is easier sometimes for the composers to work that way. After all, they know already what they are going to tell me to write and it is simpler to keep to one line at a time.

Richard Rodney Bennett, the composer, once said that he was amazed at the speed at which the music was written down on that occasion. He explained that even people who were accustomed to writing music would have difficulty in putting it down on paper with that rapidity.

But I never realise at the time it is moving so quickly. Usually it is only afterwards that I become aware of how quickly quite a considerable amount of music has been put to paper.

One last thing about the occasion when Beethoven

dictated to me for the B.B.C.—there were actually several composers present at the time, but they decided that it should be Beethoven's music that I took down at that particular time. They do seem to take it in turns to do these things, having presumably come to some arrangement.

There are only two composers of the group who have given me music that I have not yet spoken of. One is Grieg; the other Berlioz.

Grieg reminds me of a big shaggy dog. And I mean that in a very complimentary way, because I love dogs, particularly big shaggy ones!

He is very friendly and kind; warm in temperament. And I feel that he is someone with whom I could always be at ease. Rather like a very kind uncle. I feel there is an atmosphere of nature about him—and one can hear this in his music. It is the music of nature that he would want to write, and I am sure he would be very much in touch with the nature spirits.

So far, he has only given me about half-a-dozen pieces of music, none of which have been publicly performed. I would have liked to have used more than one on the first LP, but Philips decided to use just the one; a little piece called 'A Shepherd Piping'.

I see quite a lot of Berlioz because he appears to be one of Liszt's best friends. I think they were good friends in real life also, even to the extent of once sharing an apartment in Paris. At the time, Liszt was giving recitals in Paris, and Berlioz was working on a new piece of music. Liszt has told me it was *Troïlus and Cressida,* but as far as I know this opera (or it may not have been an opera) was either never finished or just not performed.

Liszt appears to be just as friendly with Berlioz as he is with Chopin, probably because they are very similar in temperament. The first time I was aware of this was on the original occasion when Liszt brought Berlioz to see me. He said: "This is my very great friend, M. Berlioz," and I could see then how much they had in common. They are very like brothers—both with a similar type of vitality and both are romantics; both full of alternate fire and dreaminess.

Also, they are very emotional people, except that Liszt has a very devout nature which is not so apparent in Berlioz.

When Berlioz first came to see me I found it difficult to communicate with him; somehow I found it almost impossible to get a good attunement. It is still not perfect, but I have had part of a march from him and snatches of orchestral music, but to date there is not one complete Berlioz composition transmitted. He seems very mercurial and not a 'sustained' communicator.

In trying to take orchestral scores from him, I'm afraid I have run into difficulties. But other than that, there isn't a great deal. In fact, I seem to see him more often than he gives me music. Mostly he just comes along with Liszt —to visit rather than to work.

Berlioz is very tall. I think he must be the tallest of all the composers who work with me, and he is quite thin, with rather sharp features. He is quite good looking with a mop of thick hair and very deep set eyes. They are very piercing eyes, so much so that when he looks hard at me I am almost inclined to shrink. He has a rather taut mouth, but there is nothing cruel about it. I would imagine it became taut with suffering from when he was on this earth.

I would like very much to receive some more music from him, and I am hopeful that the communication will improve in time. Very often it does suddenly become much clearer, though, unfortunately, I still haven't discovered what causes this to happen, so I've no way of speeding things up.

However, for the present that is the sum total of the composers who work with me. I don't think those will be the only ones to communicate though. I believe there are others 'waiting in the wings' to join the group and to communicate music. They are, of course, all welcome as far as I'm concerned. The only problem is going to be to find the time to do all that work they have planned to convey. But I hope as the months go by I will become quicker at taking down their music. And learn more about improving actual two-way communication.

CHAPTER EIGHT

Healing

There is another being from the spirit world who is very much part of my life, and who has helped me on many occasions. Yet he is not a household name like the composers and philosophers who come to my home to work through me.

This man's name is Sir George Scott-Robertson. He is a surgeon in spirit, just as he was a surgeon when he was on this earth and I have known him from the time I was a small child, though he died long before I was born.

Sir George Scott-Robertson is related to me through my mother's side of the family. He would be something like a third cousin, and my mother who had known him when she was a girl often spoke of him.

According to my mother, Sir George had made up his mind from the time he was a small boy to become a surgeon. The family had servants in those days and he would joke with the maids when he was still very young saying: "Come and do up my shoelaces and I'll cut off your leg for nothing when I'm grown up!"

He achieved his ambition to become a surgeon and went out to India with the Army. For a while he was British Ambassador at Gilgat and he was also at Chittral at the time of the siege there and subsequently wrote a book entitled *The Siege of Chittral*.

When I was in my teens and my mother and I were on closer terms, I was always talking to her about "Uncle" George, recounting what he had said and describing how he looked. She would say: "I know who you mean, but he is not your uncle. He was your grandmother's cousin."

It is through this Sir George that just occasionally I have the gift to heal. He can sometimes help people, through me, to get well when they are ill. There are times when really spectacular cures take place, but on other occasions, though I pray and pray and pray, nothing seems to happen.

This ability to heal has sometimes saved me a great deal of heartache. I can remember once when my son, Thomas, was only about three, the healing power saved him from a great deal of pain and discomfort.

Thomas had had an accident. We owned an old mangle in those days which was kept in the scullery. One early afternoon while I was clearing the table after lunch, Thomas climbed up on to the shelf where the bath was set to catch the water from the washing while it was wrung. On the mangle there was a very large screw which I believe was used to tighten the rollers and somehow Thomas slipped and caught the inside of his mouth on the point of the screw, and it pierced the roof of his mouth.

I realised he had hurt himself badly when I heard his terrible screams, and looked around to see him with blood pouring from his mouth. My first thought was to stop the bleeding as best I could, and then to get help quickly. Fortunately I had trained in First Aid in the war, so I knew how to make a pad and hold it against the wound. I did this, picked him up, put him on my lap and began to pray as hard as I could for help.

At first we were going to send my mother out to telephone for an ambulance and ask for the child to be taken to the Casualty Department at the local hospital, but as it was well after lunchtime and our own doctor had a surgery at two, I thought it would be as quick, and probably less frightening for him as well as maybe even quicker, to take him there.

I sat with him on my lap in our kitchen, holding the pad over the wound in his mouth, praying all the while, and gradually the bleeding stopped. Immediately it seemed safe to do so I dashed around to the doctor, still carrying the boy and hoping to get ahead of the queue that always formed there before surgery. I was the first to arrive, and as soon as the doctor appeared, I was able to take Thomas in and explain what had happened.

The doctor examined Thomas's mouth carefully and then asked me: "When did this happen?"

"About an hour ago," I told him.

"That's impossible," he said flatly.

I couldn't understand what he meant.

"But it *was* only an hour ago," I told him, and asked anxiously: "Is there something badly wrong?"

He shook his head a little and said: "Well, I wouldn't have believed it. The flesh has already started to heal. I could have sworn this happened at least 24 hours ago."

Happily there was nothing for him to do. Thomas and I went back home. The mouth healed completely within a day or two even though it had originally been a really deep wound.

I believe that all healing comes from one source; the life force that we call God. And I am certain that this healing power is present in all of us if we can only learn to use it, and draw upon it when it is needed. It is this force which takes over with people who have the gift to administer healing in public. And if the patient has faith in the fact that they can be healed, then half the battle is won. Our old doctor who was a very kindly man and very skilled as both a doctor and a surgeon used to say to me that he could not really help any patient who did not wish to be cured. And he added that sometimes people did not even realise that they had no desire to be made well.

I have no idea whether or not he believed in my 'faith' or spiritual healing, but he certainly understood one of the most important aspects of it. And the power to heal is not confined only to spiritual or faith healers. I believe it works to some extent through many people and also through doctors and nurses, although they are, of course, using their own skill and training as well. Some of them, without realising it, are almost certainly tuned into the life force, and perhaps it is this hidden ability that makes the difference between a wonderful nurse or doctor and those who are mediocre.

Of course, it was not I who healed Thomas. It was the life force, and the help of George Scott-Robertson. Today I also have the help of Chopin and Liszt. Both are compassionate and always say if they know that anyone is ill or in pain that they themselves will try to help.

Years ago, when I first realised that I could sometimes be used as a channel for healing, I used to work on the principle of asking very simply for assistance. I would say: "Please God, enfold this person in your healing power and may all be done that is possible to relieve their sufferings and heal them completely."

Today I work on the principle of affirmation. Instead of thinking of the affliction or ailment of a person I try to visualise him or her as being perfectly well. I still 'tune in' to the life force, of course, but I try to see the person who is suffering in God's presence and in perfect health and well-being.

Yet simple, fervent prayer can help as well. When

Georgina was about two, and before Thomas arrived on the scene, she somehow managed to get a large hooked splinter into one of her fingers.

My husband tried to take it out and so did I. We tried everything we could think of, but because it was so deeply embedded and in a 'hair-pin' shape, we simply were unable to move it.

Eventually we decided that the only thing to do was to take the child to the doctor, but until it was time for surgery I just took her in my arms and crooned her off to sleep. All the while I was thinking: "Poor little thing. A splinter in the finger can be so painful, and it's miserable to be going to the doctor for anything like that when you're small." So I began to pray for help.

I prayed for some time, and then quite suddenly, and while I was still praying, the splinter just fell out of her finger. One minute it was embedded in the flesh, the next it was lying on my lap. And how it happened, I shall never really know.

My mother had the same gift to some degree, but as in my case it would not always work for her. Nevertheless, our united prayers would sometimes achieve marvellous results.

I remember when one of the local scoutmasters was found to have cancer of the colon. The hospital X-rayed him, and found it was very bad indeed and so far advanced that he would have to have an operation. My mother was asked to pray for him, and she asked me to help as well. We prayed every night together, and when it finally became time for the man to have the operation, they X-rayed him again to discover how far the cancer had spread. They found there wasn't the slightest trace of any growth at all. How had it disappeared? We believed that God's power had accounted for it.

They discharged him and sent him home. He eventually died years later of something quite different.

I am certain that the divine power to heal is available all the time. It is all about us and within us, but we don't know how to tap it. It is rather like electricity. Always there, but you must switch it on, and, in the first place, harness it. Healers seem to be acting as a sort of connection or 'switch'.

This healing power is transmitted through healers and can be of great help to those who are suffering once it is brought to consciousness. I don't propose to understand all the principles of it, but sometimes help from other sources combined with faith and prayer can work very miraculously. But one does have failures, when there is no improvement in the patient. I myself think that in some cases this may be a blockage in the thinking of the person who is ill. Maybe they lack faith, or maybe they are so negative thinking that the life force cannot function through them or are so much in the grip of their illness or disability that they cannot be lifted out of it.

Another instance of absent healing where some help was been given concerns an actor and writer named Charles Laurence. All his life he had suffered with one weak eye muscle. This has meant that his eyes did not focus properly, and also that he continuously saw a thin black vertical line in front of the vision of the affected eye.

I volunteered to try to be a channel of help, and I 'linked up' with my 'Uncle George' and he has managed to improve Charles Laurence's condition quite considerably. Now his eyes focus better and for the first time in his life, the vertical line is no longer visible to him.

And finally one more case. Since the work with the composers began to be known I have made many new friends. One of them is Bob Bouma, who is the Press and Public Relations Officer for Philips's Recording Company in Holland.

Bob and his wife have been very kind to me on the occasions when I have visited Holland. These trips have been on business, either to take tests at the University of Utrecht, or to help with work regarding the Philips long playing record of the composers' music, and one occasion to appear and play on 'live' television at Laren.

On my first visit the Boumas were kind enough to realise that I would be more at home with friends than in an hotel, so they invited me and my son to stay with them at their house, where they treated Thomas and myself as part of the family.

However, on another visit to Holland in the summer of 1970, I arrived to find that Bob had been involved in a serious car crash, and had fractured his knee-cap. He was in hospital in a private ward, in bed with a cradle in place over the leg to keep off the weight of the blankets.

I had gone to visit him with his wife and Jan Rubinstein, another very kind man also an employee of Philips, and it was quite obvious that Bob, though trying to keep cheerful, was in considerable pain. Fortunately, my 'Uncle George', the spirit surgeon, was with me, and suggested that we might try to help.

Rather diffidently I asked Bob if he would mind if I tried to ease his pain a little. He half-smiled and said. "Go ahead. Anything that might help I would be very grateful for."

The spirit surgeon gave me my instruction.

"In order to give healing," he said, "do not touch the leg. Just hold your hands around the knee."

I did as I was told, and it was quite extraordinary. I was even surprised myself. As I stood there with my hands near, but not touching the knee, the swelling went down visibly!

Neither Bob, nor his wife, Ada, could believe their eyes. Gingerly Bob put out his hand to feel the knee himself.

"I can touch it without it hurting," he said. "And look, I can move it. I haven't been able to do that since the accident."

I think the reason that the attempt to help on that occasion was so spectacularly successful was because Bob had faith. Also he *wanted* to be healed. Had his frame of mind been different, nothing that the healing power, or 'Uncle George' did could have made the slightest bit of difference to his knee.

When people do not wish to be well, no power on earth or from the other side can function effectively. For it is only possible to act according to the unwritten law of free will.

And, of course, we do all have our allotted span. As you can imagine, when my husband was ill I prayed unceasingly. But he went. I realise now it must have been the time for him to go.

At first I was broken-hearted and missing his physical presence greatly, but then one day a friend said to me: "But your prayers were answered. He was healed. He has a new body and he is perfectly well."

My friend was quite right, of course, but in my grief at loosing our togetherness in this life, I had not been able to see his passing in that way. But I now realise that the truth is that his death was the ultimate healing—for he was very very ill indeed—and the final release from all physical suffering.

CHAPTER NINE

The Evidence

Perhaps the most difficult aspect of the work that I do with the composers is the constant pressure on me to prove the authenticity of the sources of the music. Naturally I understand that the world needs substantial proof, but producing some sort of miraculous piece of information or startling conclusive fact is not as simple as one might think.

If I get from the composers a piece of information about their life or work that is so 'exclusive' that it is not possible to verify, the sceptics immediately think that I have just made it up or imagined it. But on the other hand some piece of information that is checkable—even through a deeply obscure book or document, can lead to the accusation that I have really found out the details for myself through the available sources, and am presenting them as evidence.

It is a quite considerable problem. However, there are some incidents that have happened over the last six or so years which do help to some extent to defeat the sceptics. Though, as far as my own feelings are concerned the very solid fact of over four hundred pieces of music written down over a comparatively short period of time is probably the most incontrovertible truth of all.

I have mentioned previously the many theories that

people dream up to explain away the music. Another suggestion is that I 'suffer' from cryptomnesia—hidden memory. And yet another is that mentally all is not as it should be as far as I am concerned. Neither are true. And I am happy to be able to say that one of the world's leading authorities on Parapsychology has taken a great deal of trouble 'testing' me and the results of the tests disprove both of those theories.

The parapsychologist is Professor Doctor W. H. C. Tenhaeff, Director of the Institute of Parapsychology at the State University of Utrecht in Holland. This is the only institute of its kind in the world.

Professor Tenhaeff heads a team of experts who are far in advance of any others in research in this field, and when Philips' Recording Company brought out the first long playing disc of the composers' music, they asked if I would agree to be really thoroughly tested by the Professor and his team of experts.

After long and exacting interviews with the Professor and his colleagues, he said, regarding the theory of cryptomnesia: ". . . suffice it to point out that a scrutiny of all the data available in the matter of Rosemary Brown must lead to the conclusion that the cryptomnesia hypothesis (unconscious plagiarism) does not convincingly explain the origin of her compositions, which now number more than four hundred."

He also said in a statement to the world's press:

"The case of Rosemary Brown belongs in my opinion among those about which we shall long remain in uncertainty as to whether the spiritual hypothesis is applicable. As I said elsewhere, I do not in principle reject the hypothesis (spiritual) adhered to by Rosemary Brown and others, but non-rejection and acceptance are not synonyms. I am, however, wholly convinced that the

origin of her compositions should be made the subject of
a thorough-going investigation. The start has already been
made. Rosemary Brown was in the Netherlands a short
while ago, and we seized the opportunity of her visit to
subject her to a tentative psychological and psychiatric
examination. The result showed that we have to do with
a woman of sound mental balance, who is not in the least
anxious to occupy the limelight.

"Indeed, the contrary is rather the case. My collabor-
ator—an asylum psychiatrist of many years' experience,
was unable to find a single mental aberration, neither did
our psycho-diagnostic examination give reason to conclude
any deviation whatsoever. Meanwhile, plans are under
way for a continued investigation, in which musicologists
of repute will take part.

"Whatever the results will turn out to be as regards the
spiritualistic nature of her phenomena, I am convinced
that the investigation will lead to an important enrich-
ment of our knowledge of the so-called mediumistic
phenomena.

"Among the numerous subjects brought to my notice
in the course of a great many years, Rosemary Brown is
certainly one of the most interesting. She is also one of the
most likeable and, last but not least, one of the most level-
headed."

In a way it is not pleasant to find that one is being tested
by an asylum psychiatrist—but Liszt did warn me when
I agreed to undertake the work that just that sort of thing
was liable to happen. And at least the results of the tests
were favourable!

Perhaps as this chapter is basically about proof, it
would be best to continue in the words of other people,
and go on to David Cairns, who is an executive at Philips'
Records.

He has become a good friend of mine, and was involved on two occasions with some rather unusual incidents. He wrote down afterwards exactly what had happened. With his permission I set down here, in his own words, the background to the stories.

David writes:

"Sometime in August last year (1969) Colin Davis, Erik Smith (the producer) and I were going through the score of *The Trojans* in Erik's house and discussing various artistic and technical problems, and listening to some tapes of previous performances by Colin Davis and other conductors, and the question of the tempo of various movements naturally came up.

"Two of Berlioz's metronome struck us all as rather quick: the Septet: quaver $=$ 120, and the Love Duet: quaver $=$ 126.

"Colin Davis's tempos for these two movements were appreciably slower, and we discussed the discrepancy, Erik Smith and I feeling that Colin might possibly with advantage slightly quicken them. He said he was not averse to trying it out.

"I then half-jocularly suggested asking Rosemary Brown to try to find out Berlioz's own view on the question. I wrote to her on August 27th, 1969, and I quote from my letter: '...we wondered whether, if you have the opportunity, you could ask Liszt to ask Berlioz (or Berlioz direct), about two metronome marks in *The Trojans* which puzzle us a little. Both the tempo of the Septet (quaver $=$ 120) and the related tempo of the Love Duet (quaver $=$ 126) seem surprisingly fast. It would be interesting to hear his comments.

"A week or two later, Rosemary telephoned me at my office and said she had asked Liszt the question. His reply was that they *were* too fast. I give the words as she told me them and as I wrote them down during our telephone conversation: 'ceci soit quatre-vingt-dix, cela doit être quatre-vingt-seize.' She said she expressed her surprise at the large difference between these figures and the published ones and questioned him as to whether they were correct, to which Liszt replied very emphatically: 'J'en suis sûr.'

"Colin Davis, who was by this time in the thick of rehearsals for the Covent Garden production and had come to his own conclusions, was amused when I told him the results of our inquiry, but any suggestion that he changed his tempos in the light of them is quite untrue."

The second incident that David was involved with had to do with Monteverdi, quite the earliest of all the composers I have seen.

David writes: "On December 16th, 1969 I had lunch with Rosemary Brown at Harris's Steak House in Wembley during the recording of her piano pieces for Philips. No one else was present at our table. Our conversation was essentially relaxed, informal, spontaneous, even light-hearted.

"I had lately been playing Schubert's Grand Duo (and had become quite convinced in my own mind that, despite certain obviously 'unpianistic' features in the writing, it was a true piano work, not an orchestral work in disguise). This led me to say to Rosemary that one aspect of her work that might well develop would be the solving of notorious musicologist controversies, such as this one about the Grand Duo. She immediately answered that (I quote her own words) 'I happen to have a particularly good line of communication with Schubert today and I can tell you that it definitely isn't': i.e. isn't an orchestral work in disguise. I then said she would clearly be in great demand to find lost Schubert manuscripts: e.g. the Gastein Symphony. She said there *were* Schubert manuscripts still to be discovered in Vienna and elsewhere.

"At that I said, what about all those lost operas of Monteverdi? She answered immediately that she had just that instant seen Monteverdi (the first time she had seen him)—she described him as about her height, lean, with brown hair, heavy eyebrows, a neat pointed beard, and large ears. He was evidently a man with a ready wit. He was there with his daughter (Monteverdi is not known to have had a legitimate daughter, I understand). She had the impression that in composing he wrote not continuously, but disjointedly, in bits. He gave her a picture of a courtyard, which she described to me in great detail. I noted them down the same evening, as follows:

"A courtyard with a sunken well in the middle, with steps down to it on two sides. The courtyard had buildings on three sides, but was open on the fourth. The fourth side opened onto a street with a name something like Palazzia. The houses on the far side of this street were detached. The buildings on the right and left-hand side of the courtyard were plain, flat-roofed; on the third side there was one building, higher and more ornate, in the centre rising to a point, with one room front, one back, apparently of three stories, with small steps up to the door. This building used to be a single dwelling. To the right and left of it was a smooth stone wall, and another higher wall visible behind the house. There seemed to be fountains on either side of the courtyard, but these she could only hear, not see. Some kind of shrub was dotted around. She smelt a pungent smell, slightly sweet, like tar. The bottom left-hand corner (as you look at it) of the building was associated with Monteverdi. The top windows had projecting stone canopies.

"Names heard in connection with this picture:

"Venezia.

"Bolognese.

"This is, as I remember, everything that Rosemary Brown told me in the course of about ten minutes, before we passed to other topics."

It was odd the way Monteverdi turned up that day. I had never seen him before, but David Cairns just happened to mention him—and there he was, wearing Elizabethan clothes, puffed out sleeves with slashes in them, very elegantly dressed and with those remarkably large ears. I didn't like to say anything about them at first, because it sounds a bit rude to comment. But then I thought, he must know what I'm thinking, because they always *do* know what I'm thinking, so I said to David: "He's got awfully large ears. I don't want to be rude and offend him, but they are quite remarkable."

The mental picture Monteverdi gave me of the courtyard was very clear indeed. He took me to the far left-hand corner, and led me up to the first floor window and he said that it was in that room where he had lived and worked for a time. He also said there was quite a high wall behind the house, and it was a little way away from a canal.

Afterwards David Cairns did some research and the next time I saw him he produced a picture of Monteverdi, and there they were—the big ears. As for the missing manuscripts, Monteverdi apparently wrote in the building he showed me, but I would doubt if the music is there now. The building may not even exist today.

The Schubert thing was also rather odd. Schubert once told me that there would be some of his music found—pieces he had written when he was about 19. When I met Peter Dorling on the television programme, it occurred to me that perhaps I should tell him, but he said that the pieces had been found and the fact reported in the news-papers two or three days previous. Actually I had known for some time, and could kick myself that I had not told anyone earlier.

It was at this time that Peter Dorling asked me if I could get some information which wasn't readily avail-able, but which would help to prove the authenticity of the music for the B.B.C. programme that he was making about me. I asked Liszt if he could help, and he made the same point that I have already made—regarding the problems of producing this type of evidence.

"If it's something that is in a book," he said, "people will say you have read it, but if there is no record any-where it can't be checked. But nevertheless, I will think about it."

A few days later he came back and told me that he thought he could provide something. He then told me that in 1854, he had been to Leipzig, and whilst he was there, he had been taken ill.

"I was attended to by a Doctor Richter," he said. "Tell the gentleman from the B.B.C. about that."

Well, the first reaction from the B.B.C. was that it could not be true. Liszt, they said, had given up touring in 1848 and was unlikely to have been in Leipzig. Peter Dorling asked me if I was absolutely certain of the date, and I told him that Liszt had been quite clear. It was Leipzig, and it was 1854.

Fortunately, Peter Dorling decided to go on delving and he went to a library somewhere in Westminster, and he delved and delved in obscure books that one could not get easily in any library, and he found that Liszt did, in fact, go to Leipzig in 1854 and that he was taken ill while he was there.

There was another incident with Peter Dorling on the

occasion when I was at his home for lunch one day. Late that afternoon, Peter asked me if I could get anyone from the other side who was connected with him. Now I was very, very tired, as all through lunch Peter had been asking question after question, so much so that his wife had finally said: 'For heaven's sake let her eat her meal in peace.' My concentration had almost gone, but I did see someone—a man—and I described him, saying that I wasn't sure of the name, but that I thought it was Alfred.

Peter Dorling could not think who it could be, but when I saw him next he said: "Do you remember describing a man to me? Well, it was my grandfather. But you didn't get the name given correctly. He was called Albert."

Apparently he hadn't recognised my description as he had never actually met his grandfather, but had realised who it was from checking with other members of his family.

That was really just a small thing, but there are many others which put together do, I think, make for pretty conclusive evidence.

Peter Dorling, for example, also told me that the B.B.C. had been looking through a lot of my manuscripts and then found that the handwriting and the way the notes were written down varied between the pieces from the different composers. Almost as if I was being partly guided when I was writing down the music.

A similar thing happened when a film was made about the music for America. I noticed while watching the film at a private showing that while I was playing on the screen my eyes appear to be tightly closed all the time. I wonder really if I was 'out' then. I am never really entirely certain what is happening to me, and although I seem to be and even feel to be completely conscious I think that perhaps I am slightly 'taken over' on some occasions.

It is not necessary to be in a deep trance for automatic writing, and as far as the setting down of the music is concerned, there could be a form of automatic writing involved. A well-known pianist said that he had a facsimile of Chopin's music somewhere, and that he had noticed the way my music was put down was in exactly the same way that Chopin used in life, even to the remarks, except that I have them in English instead of French. But the phrasing was the same, and even the instructions for the repeats.

Where there was a repeat on the music—after say about a page and a half of notes, and then the beginning had to repeat, Chopin had told me: "Just put 'repeat the first eight bars'," which I did, and then he showed me how to put lines around it to draw attention to the repeat. The pianist said this was identical to the methods Chopin used when he was here on earth.

But there are, I'm sure, a lot of subtle things happening that I don't realise, and perhaps even other people don't either.

One morning when I was writing to Mary Firth, Sir Donald Tovey had come to see me, and he said: "Will you mention Felix Weingartner in your letter?"

I had a vague idea that Weingartner was a musician, but other than that the name meant nothing. Tovey spelt it out for me, and in my letter to Mary I said: "Well, Tovey wants me to mention Felix Weingartner, but I can't think why. That's all he will say."

When Mary received my letter it was at about the same time as she and her husband were in possession of some of Sir Donald's letters which had been locked away in Edinburgh at some University archives, and they were slowly wading through them.

Later that morning after receiving my letter, they began

to read some Tovey letters, and suddenly one of them mentioned Felix Weingartner. The Firths said that it was really a little too much of a coincidence for me to have mentioned the name in those circumstances, and then for them to open up a letter and read about the man.

Another time when Tovey came to see me he brought Dr. Albert Schweitzer with him. I thought the doctor was a wonderful person so I wrote and told the Firths that I had met him with Sir Donald.

They were amazed, and wrote back to say that in life Sir Donald and Albert Schweitzer had been great friends, which I most certainly hadn't known with Schweitzer living out in Africa somewhere and Tovey spending most of his life in Edinburgh.

Schweitzer gave me a little fragment of organ music— only about a page, but I think he was rather too excited about communicating, and he seemed to lose contact. Tovey told me he had written some very beautiful music, but nothing that the severe music critics would hail as supreme genius. I have never seen Schweitzer again, and I rather think that Tovey only brought him along as a friendly thing, and to let the Firths know that people can meet their friends in that next world.

Someone else who has been very kind to me is Richard Rodney Bennett, the composer. Dorothy Bacon of *Life* magazine brought him to my home because she wanted the opinion of a contemporary composer on the music. Richard played a lot of the composers' music, said he believed in it, and though it wasn't *all* good music, he felt that communication was taking place.

Having found out that he played the piano as well as composing, I said that I would like to go to one of his recitals and asked if he was giving one soon.

He said he was. And added: "I'm a bit worried about

one piece I'm playing. It is to be a recital of Debussy music, and I'm not certain of the interpretation of one of the pieces."

All he had mentioned was Debussy. I had no idea which pieces he was planning to play, but Debussy himself was delighted that the recital was taking place, and gave me quite a long, detailed description of how the piece that was bothering Richard should be tackled.

He went into it quite thoroughly, describing various passages, and saying which ones needed more pedal, and which chords should be more staccato, and so on.

It was really extraordinary because I had been given no indication at all of which piece of music was involved, and when I told Richard Rodney Bennett, he said: "That's very strange, because everything you have said could apply to the piece of music I'm concerned with. In fact, I don't think it could apply to any other piece of Debussy's."

He did, in fact, follow out the advice given by Debussy and found that it solved the problem.

Life magazine, incidentally, spent weeks investigating me. So did the B.B.C. Checking with my doctor and my neighbours. About three different sets of people have checked with my doctor because one musician suggested that I had had a thorough musical training, had amnesia and forgotten it!

I'm very fortunate really because having lived here all my life there are people who have been here for years and several families who have watched me grow up. There are still relatives alive, as well as one of my brothers. The local doctor has my medical history back to the year dot. All these different people who were investigating me asked for my permission to apply to him, which, of course, I gave. So he wrote first to *Life*, then to the B.B.C., and then to someone else. Then he finally wrote to me and said he thought it was all rather amusing because even if I had had amnesia, he couldn't see that it would explain what I was doing now.

But it is very difficult to convince some people. Mary Firth took quite a lot of my Chopin music to Dr. Hanz Gal, a very great musicologist who lives in Edinburgh. She didn't mention where the music had come from—she merely said one of her students had produced it. Which, of course, was really true, in a way. She played some of the Chopin to him, and he apparently was very enthusiastic, saying that whoever had written it had a complete absorption of Chopin. He was, in fact, amazed that anyone could have absorbed a composer so completely. According to Mary he said that whoever had written the music must have studied Chopin and played his music all her life.

All the time Mary was saying: "No. No. No." Adding, "I doubt whether the woman who produced the music could even play very much Chopin—" Which was true. She also explained that I hadn't had very much in the way of tuition or any kind of musical background."

He was so mystified, that in the end she explained to him. But he found the truth totally impossible to believe. He said categorically, "There is no after-life so that is impossible".

Fortunately there are many others who are open-minded on the subject of life after death. A professional artist, Margaret Stow, wrote to me after the music began to be known, and we have become great friends. As a present, she painted a landscape picture for me with a swan-boat in the foreground. This was to illustrate one of the pieces of music that Liszt has given me. It is a most beautiful picture and I love it—and Liszt, too, was very pleased with it.

He and I were looking at it together not long after it arrived at my home and he said casually: "I was there while she was painting it, you know. She had a lot of trouble trying to get the boat to look right and to create the light effect she wanted in the sky!

I told Margaret what he had said, and she agreed it was quite correct. He also passed on a message to her about a dearly loved dog who died—a basset hound. And added, as proof, "Tell her it is the dog who had something wrong with his left front paw when he was a puppy."

Again he was quite right. The dog had had a cyst removed from that paw when he was still quite small.

All sorts of little things like that happen. One evening I was having a splendid dinner with my agent, Barry Krost and some of his friends at the White Elephant Club in London.

Suddenly I said to Barry: "Everyone is going to laugh, but you're interested in Einstein, aren't you?"

Everyone did laugh, because Barry, though very intelligent is very modern and what I suppose would be called a 'swinging' young man. But Barry himself wasn't laughing.

"It's quite true," he said. "I am interested in Einstein. How did you know?"

"Because Einstein is here and he told me," I said, which rather stopped the conversation dead for a minute, with the party looking uneasily about them, as I find people sometimes do when something like that occurs.

On another occasion I was interviewed by Evans Senior who writes for the magazine *Music and Musicians*.

He said in passing that his grandfather had actually taken piano lessons from Liszt, and wondered if Liszt would remember. I put the question to Liszt, who said immediately: "Yes, he was the youngster with the mop of red hair."

Evans Senior had no idea whether or not his grandfather had been red-headed when young—because he only knew him during the latter years of his life—but he made enquiries around his family, and found that in fact his grandfather did have bright red hair.

This, I thought was interesting, as it disproves the theory of any kind of telepathy between me and other people. If Evans Senior had no idea that his grandfather had had red hair, he could hardly have put the thought into my mind.

There are so many puzzling things about E.S.P. You can have half-a-dozen mediums in the room and they won't all see the same people. On other occasions they will. Georgina, my daughter, and I have often seen Liszt at the same time, and we are both aware of what he is doing and exactly how he is moving. But this is rather unusual.

However, I am happy that the music is being recognised today, in spite of the many difficulties it causes me to face. And I am happy, too, when I can help someone. The Hungarian photographer (whom I have mentioned before), whose name is Tom Blau, and whose mother in spirit Liszt brought to see him—wrote me afterwards.

"I wonder whether you were aware of how deeply I was moved and stirred by what occurred towards the end of our session," he said. "I had asked whether you would be able to put me in touch with my mother and you gave me a description of her so striking and convincing that it has occupied my mind ever since."

We met again afterwards, and Liszt was able to bring Mr. Blau's father as well as his mother. And the genuineness of this was confirmed when Liszt insisted that I tell Mr. Blau that his father's name was Ludwig—but that he was always called Little Ludwig. This, according to Mr. Blau, was quite correct.

It is the music, though, and the letters like that one which for me, make this sometimes very inconvenient gift of mine all worth while. And my one hope is that one day the world will recognise the music as genuine communication so that the composers' work will not be in vain.

Here are two pages of manuscript for Valse Brilliante. It was inspired by Liszt about October, 1967.